Praise for My

Jenn Hand is the encourager we all n[...]
(but still so fun) voice we long for or [...] ...er words
come alongside you wherever you are today and help you step into more of
God's best for you!

HOLLEY GERTH, bestselling author of *The Powerful Purpose of Introverts:
Why the World Needs You to Be You*

I just absolutely adore how honest Jenn is about all the reasons we don't want
to put our "Yes" on the table: "What if God calls me to something too big?"
"What if God calls me to do something I'll hate?" But . . . "What if I put my
yes on the table and it's more than I could ever imagine?" You, my friend,
don't want to live a half-life. And that is not God's plan for your one, precious
life. Let Jenn show you how to put that yes on the table.

KATHI LIPP, bestselling author of *The Husband Project* and *Clutter Free,*
coauthor of *An Abundant Place,* and founder of The Red House Writers

Jenn Hand has long been someone I consider a favorite human, but now I see
her as one of my new favorite authors. *My Yes Is on the Table* is encouraging. It's
spiritually deep. It's practical. It's well laid out and a beautiful mix of story and
Bible. This book feels like a friend sitting across from you, helping you as you
place your own yes on the table.

SUZANNE ELLER, bestselling author, founder of TogetHER Ministries,
and cohost of *More Than Small Talk* podcast

Do you long for more in your walk with God? Does it feel like God is calling
you to something too big or too hard? Is fear stopping your yes? If these questions reflect what's in your heart, I invite you to take an amazing, fun-filled,
faith-shaking, life-transforming adventure with my friend Jenn Hand through
her new book, *My Yes Is on the Table.* Through God's Word and some amazing
tales of her own, she'll guide you step by step, story by story, to trust God with
your yes, bringing famous friends like Moses and Joshua along on the journey.
Don't miss the more God has for you. Don't give in to the fear that stops you.
Instead, join Jenn and walk confidently and courageously into the yes God has
for you. He's waiting for you on the other side!

WENDY BLIGHT, author; Proverbs 31 Ministries Biblical Content Specialist

My only challenge in reading Jennifer Hand's new book, *My Yes Is on the Table,*
was pacing, because I definitely wanted to read it all in one sitting! Who doesn't
love adventure stories? Combine the courageous, often upside-down world of

God using and guiding His people several millennia ago, with the spontaneous and joyful spirit of this trauma counselor, speaker, author, and cheerleader, and the result is wonder, wit, and great wisdom for your own life. Jennifer will not let you hold on to fear, regret, or excuses—she calls us all into the totally surrendered life of fully following Jesus and pouring into other hungry souls along the way. Her delightfully unique voice and laughter echoed as I thoroughly embraced my own best *yes* in response to her words. Read this book, and then tell me all the amazing things that you truly believe God can do. *In* you. *Through* you. All that is required is your own *yes*.

LUCINDA SECREST MCDOWELL, author of *Soul Strong* and *Life-Giving Choices*

Few books have transformed my life like *My Yes Is on The Table*. It has challenged me to trust God more, encouraged me to respond with quick obedience, and inspired me to believe in the power of the Spirit of God at work in my life. Fear was put in its proper place and replaced by faith. This message will unlock an adventure with God you cannot imagine is possible. An adventure where your heart cries "Yes" even before you know the next step to take because you've grown to fully rest in His promises.

DR. SAUNDRA DALTON-SMITH, physician, author, and host of *I Choose My Best Life* podcast

Jennifer draws the curtain back on the puppet show that is fear—exposing the enemy's attention-seeking scripts. *My Yes Is on the Table* cuts the strings on fear so that all of us can live a life full of God's blessings.

KAT ARMSTRONG, Bible teacher and author of *No More Holding Back* and *The In-Between Place*

After doctors told me I would die if I didn't quit drinking, I knelt by the couch I was living on and prayed to Jesus: "I have squandered everything You've given me, but whatever I have left . . . it's Yours." It was that YES that radically changed my life. If ever you've wondered, *Could God do something in and through my life?* the answer in Christ is YES—and your YES is how God will move YOU into just that. God is always after His glory and our good—and He delights to accomplish His will through His people . . . but not all His people are willing. Jennifer Hand's *My Yes Is on the Table* is the heart-changing, life-changing, and eternity-changing spark you need to give God permission to set your faith on fire.

JOHN ELMORE, author of *Freedom Starts Today* and Teaching Pastor of Watermark Community Church in Dallas, TX

MY YES
IS ON THE
TABLE

MOVING FROM
FEAR TO FAITH

JENNIFER HAND

MOODY PUBLISHERS

CHICAGO

Edited by Pamela Joy Pugh
Interior design: Brandi Davis
Cover design: Erik M. Peterson
Cover illustration of table copyright © 2020 by Alina1888 / Shutterstock (1718733739). All rights reserved.
Author photo: BT Photography

ISBN: 978-0-8024-2558-4

Originally delivered by fleets of horse-drawn wagons, the affordable paperbacks from D. L. Moody's publishing house resourced the church and served everyday people. Now, after more than 125 years of publishing and ministry, Moody Publishers' mission remains the same—even if our delivery systems have changed a bit. For more information on other books (and resources) created from a biblical perspective, go to www.moodypublishers.com or write to:

Moody Publishers
820 N. LaSalle Boulevard
Chicago, IL 60610

1 3 5 7 9 10 8 6 4 2

Printed in the United States of America

For my parents, Mike and Vicky Hand, who taught me all about Jesus around our always fun table.

Michelle, Todd, Alex, Hope, Abbi, and Jacob Ray for letting me be part of your table.

Contents

1

Standing on
the Edge

I WAS SITTING CROSS-LEGGED on my a-little-bit-too-tiny bed
in Kathmandu, Nepal, as I listened online to Beth Moore teaching. I had to sit cross-legged because I had the bed custom made
when I first moved to Nepal, and the measurements somehow
got lost in translation. The cutest bed looked like it could be in a
Pottery Barn magazine, but it was doll-sized.

I am not doll-sized.

Beth Moore asked a question in this message that I could not
get out of my heart: "Where does your mind spew?" I knew the
answer instantly. I was afraid God would ask me to leave Nepal. I
had said yes to serving Him overseas. I had done emotional good-
byes at the airport. So emotional that the tiny airport in my town
called security because so many were gathered around me crying
as if they were sending me off to my funeral.

I was appointed to be a career missionary. When you take an
assignment as a career missionary, you typically commit to a long-
term career of service in missions overseas versus a short-term trip
for a few weeks or a few years. I dreamed that I would live so long

in Nepal that someday they would name something after me like they did the Lottie Moon Christmas offering. I had placed my yes before the Lord, and here I was on the doll bed that day, realizing my greatest fear was that an obedient yes to God would mean no to what I thought I was to "do" for Him.

Let's pause here. Maybe you are reading this and thinking, "One of the main reasons I don't want to say yes to God is because He might call me to live in a remote village in the outermost parts of the world, and I would not have access to Amazon Prime when I need my favorite brand of coffee creamer."

We all have different fears of placing our yes on the table before the Lord. Mine may be different than yours, but both of us can stand on the edge of the adventure to our promised land and want to say no because fear stops us in our tracks.

I had known for a while that the Lord was speaking to my heart that He had more than one place and people for me to serve. Every sermon I heard for months centered around obedience. We studied the life of Abraham. In Genesis 12, God told Abraham to go to a land that He would show him. As I prayed, I knew God was calling me to be willing to not stay in Nepal but keep going to the lands God would show me.

The more I prayed and tried to get brave enough to listen, the more I sensed a different direction in my life than remaining in one country as a missionary. I had known since I was a young girl and forced the kids to come to my Bible club on the playground that I came alive teaching God's Word to others.

I had a counseling degree and a passion for people to experience healing and hope. What if I could travel the world inviting people to come alive in Christ through teaching His Word and providing counseling and written resources? What if this was my mission?

(Spoiler Alert: This yes to God was how Coming Alive Ministries formed!)

But I was afraid to listen to that leading. I had worked too hard to learn *this* language. To learn how to teach a Bible study and use the right word for fear in the Nepalese language, because there may or may not have been that one time I led a whole Bible study on fear and wondered why the women were giggling the entire time. (It turns out, the word for *diarrhea* and *fear* are *very* similar in the Nepalese language.) I had wrapped my identity up in being a single missionary willing to serve. What would people think? Fear of looking like a failure consumed me. Partner that with a fear of rejection.

Fear of the next and what this would mean for the now. Fear of what my supporters would say. Fear of the unknown. Fear of "am I hearing God right?"—because I thought I heard His voice tell me to come here in the first place.

You may not find yourself sitting cross-legged on a miniature-sized bed across the world, but you have experienced some fear stops. Fill in this blank.

I want to say yes to God but I am afraid of

We have some friends in the Bible who were on a journey of obedience to their promised land. They were following God with their yes and standing on the edge of their promised land.

Let's become friends with this large group of people. The Israelites.

STANDING ON THE EDGE

Those poor Israelites. They had stood on the edge of their promised land–living once before. They were right there. So close. Let me catch you up in case you are new to the story. You might remember that God's people had been living in Egypt and had been forced into slavery for four hundred years. But in His timing, God heard their cries and called Moses to lead the people out. The Israelites embarked on a miraculous journey toward freedom—toward their promised land.

God had this land of promise ready for them—and He had a plan for the journey of deliverance for them. He used Moses to lead His people on this crazy improbable journey. From the parting of the Red Sea to providing manna—a miraculous meal that fell from heaven every day to feed them—there were numerous miracles along the way.

You can read about all this in the book of Exodus.

I imagine the people might have wanted the journey to their promised land to take a shorter passage. I don't know about you, but when I pick a route on my GPS, I always click the fastest way to where I am going.

Have you ever gone on a camping trip? Can you imagine camping for years as you wandered around the wilderness on the way to this new home country you had been promised? Not just staying at one campsite, but putting up and pulling down and going on the move again. Imagine camping with all of your relatives (including Great Aunt Myrtle, who always liked to pinch your cheeks and ask you why you were not married yet), your closest friends, and that person who drives you crazy because she is constantly posting selfies on social media. I am sure there would be times when you wanted to say to Julie the Instagrammer, "Could you please stop trying to get the perfect picture of your manna and just eat it before it molds already?"

Cue the rise in the background music for dramatic effect as we come to Numbers 13. The people were on the edge of the promised land, Canaan. Let's join them.

The LORD spoke to Moses, saying, "Send men to spy out the land of Canaan, which I am giving to the people of Israel. From each tribe of their fathers you shall send a man, every one a chief among them."

Moses sent them to spy out the land of Canaan and said to them, "Go up into the Negeb and go up into the hill country, and see what the land is, and whether the people who dwell in it are strong or weak, whether they are few or many, and whether the land that they dwell in is good or bad, and whether the cities that they dwell in are camps or strongholds, and whether the land is rich or poor, and whether there are trees in it or not. Be of good courage and bring some of the fruit of the land." Now the time was the season of the first ripe grapes. (vv. 1–2, 17–20)

Here is their chance to actually see their promised land. They come back with a report of trembling. Have you ever had someone ask you if you want the good news or the bad news first? They tell the good news first. The land is flowing with milk and honey. However.

It's the *however* they added that changed everything.

"However, the people who dwell in the land are strong, and the cities are fortified and very large. And besides, we saw the descendants of Anak there. . . . And there we saw the Nephilim (the sons of Anak, who come from the Nephilim), and we seemed to ourselves like grasshoppers, and so we seemed to them." (vv. 28, 33)

Ten of the twelve spies brought only the bad news. Joshua and Caleb disagreed, believing the Israelites could take the land as the Lord had promised.

Because of their anxiety-ridden report from the ten, though, panic spread quickly among the people. They lost sight of the Promise Keeper. They started to grumble among themselves and talk about how they wished they had either stayed in the slavery of Egypt or died in the wilderness. They said, "Let us choose a leader and go back to Egypt." They stood on the edge of their promised land, and their faith steps became fear stops.

These fear stops led to God telling the people that they would not see the promised land, that none who had seen what God had done for them in Egypt and as they traveled in the wilderness would get to go live in the land He has promised to them (Num. 14:22–23). Only Joshua and Caleb of their generation would enter the promised land. The others would keep wandering in the wilderness for forty years.

> They stood on the edge of their promised land, and their faith steps became fear stops.

It can be easy for me to get all judgy on the Israelite people. Why did you blow it, friends? Why couldn't you remember that the One who promised the promised land had the plan? Why did you let fear stop you?

But then I think about how fear stops me. I want to say yes to God. I want to take an obedient journey to the promised land He has for me, but I find myself stuck in fear along the way. Fears of rejection, fears of failure, concerns of "can I trust the character of God?" Feeling like a grasshopper looking at a whole bunch of giants. I can find myself grumbling and complaining. Bondage and my plan seem more comfortable. I, for one, want to stand on the edge of my promised land *and go in.*

PUT ALL YOUR CARDS ON THE TABLE

I am not a card shark. I love to play games, but I forget all the different rules for card games. If you play a game with me where I have to bluff and pretend I have things in my hand that I don't—don't ask me to be your partner. I always giggle or turn bright red or blurt out, "That's not what I have!" If I were good at bluffing, I would be attempting to deceive my opponent about what was in my hand.

If I were to lay all my cards on the table, those around me would know what was actually in my hand. I looked up what it means to put all your cards on the table. The Cambridge dictionary online records the definition as this: "To be honest about your feelings and intentions."[1] What if I intend to lay the "Yes" card before the Lord? What if I let go of the other cards in my hand and place that one down?

Yes—I will take the journey with You to the promised land that You have for me. I will take obedient faith steps even when my doubt wants me to stop. I will not stand on the edge of the promised land and take back my yes because I see some giants, and I feel like a grasshopper.

But what do I do with the fears? The wanting to throw down the "no card" tantrums that can find their way to my heart. Or where I give up and run the other way. How do I handle the unknowns of the promised land? Let's stand at the edge and follow Joshua's journey as he leads the next round of the Israelites to the promised land.

TAKE TWO

Sure, they were uneasy. They had questions. But as we take a deep dive through this book, we will find that the Israelites spied out the promised land and, instead of letting their fear stop them, they continued in their yes steps, following as the Lord led until it was time for the next generation to take the faith steps into the land of promise.

Will we get it right always? No. Will we have *what* it takes? We don't, but we have *who* it takes. What does the future hold for our journey? Let's admit together that we have some fears. We have some questions. But I want to stand on the edge, throw down my yes, and get ready to do whatever it takes to go in. Can we throw our yes on the table? I cannot wait to hear *your* stories of how you move from fear to faith.

Lay down your yes card and tell the enemy you are calling his bluff. You are going to the promised land.

YOUR YES STORY

When did you first say yes to Jesus? How did you sense Him inviting you to Himself? And if you have not said yes to Jesus, today can be your day. Say "yes" to His invitation to forgive you of your sins, your inability to reach God in your own strength. Thank Him that He reached out for you instead, coming to walk on the earth and die through crucifixion on a cross. That small three-letter word "yes" can change everything. When you said yes to Jesus, you invited His glory into your story. That yes to eternal life changes everything about our everyday lives. Our yes gives us a salvation story, but it does not stop there. Accepting Jesus' invitation to life offers the opportunity for us to be a servant for His glory.

> *You are my friends if you do what I command you. No longer do I call you servants, for the servant does not know what his master is doing; but I have called you friends, for all that I have heard from my Father I have made known to you. You did not choose me, but I chose you and appointed you that you should go and bear fruit and that your fruit should abide, so that whatever you ask the Father in my name, he may give it to you. (John 15:14–16)*

Sometimes I can find it easy to trust Jesus with my eternal life but struggle to trust Him with my everyday life. If I place my yes on the table before Him, what will He ask of me? Will I have the requirements for the journey? And what if placing my yes on the table before Him takes me to a completely different destination than I had planned?

STANDING WITH JOSHUA

Let's fast-forward. Years had passed. Moses has died, and Joshua was put in place as the leader of the people. I imagine Joshua was nervous about his yes steps. There they were on the edge of the promised land again. Will it be second-verse-the-same-as-the-first? Or a different story this time? God said to Joshua,

> *"Moses my servant is dead. Now therefore arise, go over this Jordan, you and all this people, into the land that I am giving to them, to the people of Israel. Every place that the sole of your foot will tread upon I have given to you, just as I promised to Moses." (Josh. 1:2–3)*

I believe God knew Joshua would be afraid. He tells him several times, "Be strong and courageous." Joshua 1:9 says, "Have I not commanded you? Be strong and courageous. Do not be frightened, and do not be dismayed, for the LORD your God is with you wherever you go."

Scared or not, Joshua put his yes before the Lord. In Joshua 1:10–11, we find Joshua telling the people the next steps. He told them to get ready, because in three days they would cross the Jordan River and begin to take the land God was giving them.

I love how he casually mentioned crossing over the Jordan like it was no big deal to have a giant river-crossing ahead.

He is all in. The people are all in. They are standing on the edge and ready to go in.

Let's go along for the journey with them.

WHAT IS YOUR PROMISED LAND?

The Israelites knew what their promised land was. It was an *actual* land. They were people who had been rescued from the bondage of slavery in Egypt and were on a journey to take the land that God had promised them.

What is your promised land? Besides heaven, of course. Because that is the ultimate promised land, but what about here on earth? Unlike the Israelites, we are not a large people group camping through the wilderness following a pillar of fire and a cloud. But we do find ourselves at crossroad decision points. Some choices feel like big massive life-changing decision points. Some are smaller everyday choices.

As I write this book, I am writing for the reader who is at a crossroads. Are you wondering about your next steps? Decisions like should I say yes or no to this relationship? Should I consider a job change or stay where I am? Should I put my kids in this type of schooling? Should I go to this school? Should we change churches? Can I say yes to this ministry calling? What about the crazy amount of decisions that come with being a parent? Or the heartbreaking decisions that come with caring for an aging parent? You are not just making decisions for yourself—

> Big and little moments: we stand at the crossroads of decisions. We wonder what will lead us to the promised land. Promised land–living is a life of following Him.

you are making decisions for others. What about the empty-nester figuring out her purpose in life now that the kiddos have flown the nest?

Standing in the now and trying to make the best decision for the next—that is a crossroads. The list of choices could go on and on. Even daily little decisions. Today, will I make that phone call I have been dreading, or not? Will I make the healthy food choices that I have been desperately trying to make, or eat my feelings in the brownie batter that I was preparing for Bible study tonight? Might as well add here, will I choose to exercise and take care of my body even though I want to stay snuggled in my bed instead?

Big and little moments: we stand at the crossroads of decisions. We wonder what will lead us to the promised land. Promised land–living is a life of following Him. It is obedience to Him. It is following the path marked out by Him.

> *You make known to me the path of life;*
> *in your presence there is fullness of joy;*
> *at your right hand are pleasures forevermore. (Ps. 16:11)*

The Hebrew word for path here in Psalm 16:11 is *ōrăḥ*, which means *the way or course of conduct*.[2] This sounds like promised land–living to me. Knowing the way I should go, and finding the fullness of joy in His presence as I go. Standing at the edge of the next steps as I wait in the now, placing my yes before Him to follow Him on the path of life.

The crossroads I am standing at today:

Now the question is: How do I know which way will lead to my promised land? What if I make the wrong choice? I want to say yes to God, but how will I know which way to follow God?

On their journey to the promised land, we are told in Numbers 9 that the Israelite people had set up the tabernacle, which was covered by a cloud. And then, in the evening it looked like fire covering it. Let's talk about how amazing that is.

How would you feel about approaching a church that was covered with a giant cloud? And then as evening came, that cloud morphed into a what looked like fire that encased the building? Are you picturing Disney World effects? That's what is playing on the movie of my mind right now.

> *So it was always: the cloud covered it by day and the appearance of fire by night. And whenever the cloud lifted from over the tent, after that the people of Israel set out, and in the place where the cloud settled down, there the people of Israel camped.*
>
> *Even when the cloud continued over the tabernacle many days, the people of Israel kept the charge of the LORD and did not set out.*
>
> *At the command of the LORD they camped, and at the command of the LORD they set out. They kept the charge of the LORD, at the command of the LORD by Moses. (Num. 9:16–17, 19, 23)*

They followed the presence of God. Are you thinking what I am thinking? Sure. This sounds great when you have a giant fluffy cloud and pillar of fire to follow! Where is my cloud? Where is my fire? (Well, I have started a few fires in my day accidentally, but I am not sure the presence of God was there telling me where to go. Especially that one time I burned down the only outhouse in a village.)

We may not have a cloud or a pillar of fire, but we do have some powerful promises.

> *"These things I have spoken to you while I am still with you. But the Helper, the Holy Spirit, whom the Father will send in my name, he will teach you all things and bring to your remembrance all that I have said to you." (John 14:25–26)*

We have the person of the Holy Spirit:

> *"When the Spirit of truth comes, he will guide you into all the truth, for he will not speak on his own authority, but whatever he hears he will speak, and he will declare to you the things that are to come." (John 16:13)*

We have the power of God's Word:

> *For the word of God is living and active, sharper than any two-edged sword, piercing to the division of soul and of spirit, of joints and of marrow, and discerning the thoughts and intentions of the heart. (Heb. 4:12)*

> *All Scripture is breathed out by God and profitable for teaching, for reproof, for correction, and for training in righteousness. (2 Tim. 3:16)*

We have the person and power of Jesus. The power of Jesus, which broke the chains of sin and death to come to our rescue and take us to our ultimate promised land, the heaven He left to walk the streets of earth. And we have the people of God to help us discern the path of God. Those are some powerful p's!

WHAT IF I MAKE THE WRONG CHOICE?

There are times we fear making the wrong choice because we worry that we are not hearing from God. What if I am making this decision, but I am hearing God wrong? What if I am just listening for what I *want* to hear God say instead of discerning *how* He is leading? What if I make the wrong choice? Does the Lord set options before us that we really could choose either and still find our promised land?

Let's start with the fear of hearing God wrong. There is a *big* difference between that and not waiting to listen to the Lord and instead coming up with our own plan or not seeking the Lord for His plan.

Are you afraid you are not hearing God's direction clearly or correctly? That you will miss it? I love the promise found in James 1:5: "If any of you lacks wisdom, let him ask God, who gives generously to all without reproach, and it will be given him." What a promise for this fear of making the wrong choice!

Let's talk about when we know the choice that we need to make, and we willingly choose the other.

Raise your hand, if like me, you have been there and done that, and thought the old sounded better than the new God was doing. Looked to something else or someone else for protection instead of God's direction. The Hebrews did that when they got to complaining and thinking they'd been better off in Egypt.

Here is the key to those wrong choices.

For thus said the LORD GOD, the Holy One of Israel,
"In returning and rest you shall be saved;
in quietness and in trust shall be your strength."
But you were unwilling. (Isa. 30:15)

Returning. Returning to the one who took us from Egypt in the first place. Verse 18 in that same chapter says, "Therefore the LORD waits to be gracious to you, and therefore he exalts himself to show mercy to you." What an incredible God that we have. A God who is waiting to be gracious to us even when we are wandering around in our own choices, not looking for His direction or protection.

Are you reading those paragraphs above feeling like you have been wandering around trying to find your way back to the bondage of your past, yet you have a sense of hope that God has more for you in your present and future? Return to Him.

You could take a moment even now and pray. Tell God that you have been seeking shelter in the wrong places. Maybe it is in a person. Perhaps it is in a place. Perhaps it is what felt comfortable in your past. Thank Him that He longs to be gracious to us. Then ask Him for the strength to make the *right* choice. "Your ears shall hear a word behind you, saying, 'This is the way, walk in it'" (Isa. 30:21).

MOUNT NEBO

I am freshly back from a life-changing journey where placing my yes on the table took me to the Middle East on a short-term trip with Coming Alive Ministries to serve for a few weeks, ministering to refugees displaced by war.

So freshly back that I still have that major jet lag fog so I feel like when I turn my head, it takes a while for my brain to catch up to my body, and I am waking up at three in the morning ready to go.

Did you know that you can claim jet lag as an excuse for anything you do or say that doesn't make sense for at least two weeks? At least that is what I tell myself!

Even in the jet lag fog, I wanted to write this section because I did not want too much time to pass before telling you what it was like to stand on Mount Nebo. The Mount Nebo that Moses stood on and looked over the promised land.

This trip contained a great deal of fear for me. It just so happened that at the time this trip was planned, things in the Middle East heated up more than usual. The daily news was not portraying a picture that this was a time to be hopping on a plane and going. I had to do a great deal of extra praying for discernment because I was daily getting the emails/texts/calls of people telling me they did not think I should go.

> I do not want to just look at the promised land God has for me with my eyes. I want to stand in it, dance in it, bring glory to God as I walk in it.

As I prayed, I sensed God saying, "go afraid," so I went. I found out that on our day off, we would have the chance to journey from the plains of Moab to the top of Mount Nebo. The place where Moses looked over the land that had been promised. You can read a description of what he saw in Deuteronomy 34:1–4.

I stood on this mountain and tried to imagine looking at all this through Moses' eyes. I was grateful for the helpful signs for the folks like me who cannot tell east from west or north from south.

I tried to lick my finger and stick it up in the air because I remember my dad telling me that's how you could find the North, but let's be honest, I had no idea what I was doing.

The sign showed which direction Jericho was. The place where Joshua's spies would go first to spy out the land. I looked out over the promised land and wondered what it must have felt like for Moses to know he was not going there. The team I was serving with circled up and read from Deuteronomy 34. We discussed how we felt about the fact that Moses did not get to go in.

It is hard to struggle with this. To understand the consequences of fear and disobedience. Fear and disobedience had stopped them. Friends, I do not want to just look at the promised land God has for me with my eyes. I want to stand in it, dance in it, bring glory to God as I walk in it.

What if my yes is what keeps me on the journey toward the promised land He has for me? What if your yes is what keeps you on the journey toward the promised land He has for you?

Let's place our yes on the table and continue the journey to the promised land.

I want us to do this adventure together. I would love for you to grab a piece of paper or whatever your creative mind comes up with and write the word YES. I have written YES in the sand before, the dirt, on my mirror, on a journal page—as a reminder of my yes I am placing on the table.

I would love for you to write your yes and take a picture and post it on social media using #myyesisonthetable so that we can pray over each other on this adventure of yes to God.

MY YES PRAYER

Jesus, I am here. I do not want to hold my cards tight and let the enemy see me bluffing.

I want to lay my hands open and lay one card on the table.

The Yes card.

I want to say yes to You. Yes to where You say go, do, in the big and the small. I want to take the yes journey to the promised land that You have for me.

Lord, here are my hands and my heart. Take my yes and do more than I could ever ask or imagine.

I pray You help me say yes, even when afraid. Even when I stand on the edge of the promised land and there are obstacles in the way. I say yes Lord, yes.

HEART WORK

Read Joshua 1, Deuteronomy 34:1–4, and Isaiah 43.

What is God speaking to your heart as you read?

What is one fear stop currently on your heart?

What faith step will you pray about taking?

2

Giants, Grasshoppers, and a Thread of Hope

I THINK I COULD BE a camp counselor for life. I love every cheesy bit of it. The cheers. The games. The singalongs—all the things. I started my camp counselor career at the ripe old age of twelve, when I worked at a camp for adults with special needs, some of whom also had physical disabilities. It was my favorite part of the summer. These adults taught me so much. They were full of so much joy and brought me much joy.

In the summer of my freshman year of college, I applied to work at a camp for the entire summer. I wanted that job so badly that when the camp director asked me in my interview if I would be willing to also be a lifeguard at the camp, I said, "Of course!" No, I was not thinking that would involve having to take swim tests to prove that you can save someone. I was thinking about how I would be living my best life as a summer camp counselor. I also thought I might meet the love of my life there—I mean, could there be a better-case scenario?

The director hired me and then asked me to come to camp training a week early for a lifeguard training camp. I will never forget that first day when they asked us to jump in the Olympic-sized pool and "swim a 500" using specific strokes. Five hundred what? I mean, sure, I could swim and keep myself afloat, but I did not know how to do the butterfly or the backstroke.

Somehow, I miraculously passed that section of the lifeguard test. But then there was my nemesis. They throw a brick down in the fourteen feet of water and expect you to be able to dive down and get that brick and bring it up. I was never good as a kid at the throw-the-diving-stick-in-the-water-and-get-it challenge, and this brick situation was no different.

The entire life-guarding class was cheering me on! One of my friends boldly proclaimed, "In the name of Jesus, Jenn is going to get that brick!" I think the hand of Jesus did give me that brick because there is no way I could have gone that deep, and I have never been able to again.

I feel that for the safety-conscious among us, you are worried about my passing that test and actually becoming a lifeguard. Don't worry. They quickly realized that I was not the one to watch over the deep end, so my assignment was the shallow end and the kiddie pool area. I held that lifeguard buoy with pride. Because I was a lifeguard that summer, I got placed in water week for camp. The problem was that none of the campers who had signed up for water week liked water.

As you can imagine, that made for—shall we say—an "interesting" week.

These were not your wilderness-loving middle school girls. For some reason, the camp numbers were at a capacity that week, so we did not end up sleeping on cots in the usual bunkhouses. We were assigned sleeping bags in the chapel basement. I tried to convince the middle school girls this was fun. I honestly did.

They weren't buying it.

We were settled down in our sleeping bags when all of a sudden, in the darkness, came hordes of camel crickets. Friends, have you ever seen camel crickets? They do not chirp, like other crickets. They just come.

Pause here and google an image of them. Did I mention these crickets have particularly long hind legs and beady eyes? Now that you see what they look like, join me in the basement with middle school girls squealing in their sleeping bags. These crickets became giants to them. In the darkness, they seemed to forget that they were bigger than these crickets. They could have squashed them. These girls had images of a plague of biblical proportions, and these crickets were going to eat them alive.

If I am completely honest, I found myself disgusted as well. Something about being kissed by crickets in my sleep did not make me lie down with peaceful dreams. I tried to convince the campers in my most cheerful camp counselor voice that this would be okay. Everything is fine.

But eventually, we packed up the sleeping bags and went upstairs to the chapel. We slept in the chapel for the rest of that week. The crickets won.

OVERWHELMED BY THE GIANTS

In Numbers 13, we found out about Moses sending spies into Canaan, the land promised. We talked about this a bit in chapter 1, but let's take a deeper dive here. You'll remember that God told Moses to send spies to check out this land, "which I am giving to the people of Israel" (v. 2).

Who was giving the land to the people of Israel? The God who had been guiding them. The God who had been providing for them. The God who had journeyed with them. I am glad I was not among the group that God was sending in to be a spy. I am terrible about being incognito about anything. If I'm invited to your surprise party, I'd probably end up ruining it because I'd jump out at the wrong time.

I remember trying to smuggle Bibles into a closed country. I had such high hopes of being like the famous missionaries I had read about in the past. I was putting my life on the line to bring God's Word to those in desperate need! I was the leader of a group of college students and had trained them how to handle customs upon arrival in the country. I had taught them what to do and how to interact.

> These spies saw giants. And because they saw giants, they began to see themselves as grasshoppers.

Guess what? All the college students I was with got their Bibles through.

Me? The customs guy asked me if I was bringing in any religious materials, and I found my head bobbing up and down before I could stop it, and next thing you know, all those Bibles were in the hands of the airport officials. I like to think I was evangelizing the airport.

Back to the spies.

Moses sent them to spy out the land of Canaan and said to them, "Go up into the Negeb and go up into the hill country, and see what the land is, and whether the people who dwell in it are strong or weak, whether they are few or many, and whether the land that they dwell in is good or bad, and whether the cities that they dwell in are camps or strongholds, and whether the land is rich or poor, and whether there are trees in it or not. Be of good courage and bring some of the fruit of the land." (Num. 13:17–20)

The twelve men returned from spying out the land and talked of the land flowing with milk and honey. But then ten of them talked about the giants. That summer at camp, we were surrounded by crickets who seemed like giants. That was all the girls could see. The crickets ran us out from where we were sleeping to find shelter in the chapel. These spies didn't see crickets. They saw giants. And because they saw giants, they began to see themselves as grasshoppers. Small. Defenseless. Able to be squashed by the giants.

The spies quickly forgot who had promised to give them the land because they were overwhelmed by the giants in the land.

YOUR GIANTS

What are the giants in your land that make you afraid to say yes to God? If we are gut-level honest, we sometimes forget that He is trustworthy. His plans for us are good. He is good, and He is the one that is leading us.

Do you see a financial giant? Giant bills and a tiny bank account? Are you wondering how this could be close to leading to a promised land?

Do you see the giant of the fear of failure? Every year I fill out the PowerSheets goal-setting planner by Lara Casey. In the pre-work leading up to setting my goals, they have a page that asks you to examine the fears that keep you from setting goals. Fears can become huge giants.

In the 2017 PowerSheets planner, on the "meet your fears" page, it says this:

> Fear can hold us back from making what matters happen. Write your honest feelings here. Challenge yourself to write the things you may not want to write. Why? Seeing your fears in writing can help you meet them and move forward.

Your fears do not define who you are. Name them. You can do it.[3]

Then it said, "I am afraid of _____" and left blank space to fill in. I decided that I would write down the first thing that came to my mind and heart. Here are the giants that I realized I was seeing.

The first fill-in-the-blank. "I am afraid of success in ministry or relationships because it adds a weight of expectation, and sometimes I am afraid that it will require more than I want to give."

The second fill-in-the-blank. "I am afraid of failure because failure says to me I am not enough; I cannot live up to the expectation; I should not have even tried."

I quickly realized that I would stay paralyzed and stuck between these two giants: fear of success and fear of failure. I was unable to move into the journey of placing my yes on the table to God because I was staring at two giants of fear instead.

As the spies said, I realized that I had become like a grasshopper, shrinking back and small because of these giants. But then there was this question.

"If I were to step into this fear and take action, my life would not be _____."

My fill-in-the-blank answer said this, "My life would not be stuck in the safe zone of staying in between my fear of success and fear of failure."

Now it's your turn. How would you answer those questions?

I am afraid of _____.

If I were to step into this fear and take action, my life would not be _____.

What giants have made you feel like a grasshopper?

SPY OUT THE LAND

It's that time again. It's time to spy out the land. As we talked about last time, the whole spy out the land thing didn't work out well for the Israelites. Will this be a repeat story? If this were a Netflix series on the Israelites, here is the part where I would be holding my breath. (By the way, I think this would be a good drama. Let's be honest. They spent years camping in the wilderness together, so there had to be some dramatics.) To review the action a bit, by this point Moses has died, and of the generation that originally left Egypt, everyone age twenty and older has died except for Joshua and Caleb (Num. 14:22–30).

> *And Joshua the son of Nun sent two men secretly from Shittim as spies, saying, "Go, view the land, especially Jericho." (Josh. 2:1)*

Will they see the giants and come back like grasshoppers?

I want you to picture yourself in a time when you have had to go out and "spy out the land." It will be a different scenario for each of you. A different time of life. A different land. But we have these moments where we stand before the next place, thing, person, or purpose that God is calling us to, and we are studying the situation. When you spy out the land, what do you see?

Remember when I was sitting cross-legged on the miniature bed back in chapter 1? When I spied out the land of "going back to America," I spent months only seeing the giants. The giant of what would I do if I did not carry the title

> Does anyone else feel like clapping your hands wildly here? They moved from fear to faith.

of super missionary Jenn who seemed to come with a superhero cape, staying in Nepal for decades?

The giant of fear of people thinking I was a failure who did not have what it takes. The fear of hearing, "I told you so."

The fear of what in the world happens next?

It took *months* of wrestling with these fears before I finally placed my yes on the table to take the next steps of the journey to the land God was calling me to. Back to the land where I had started. The spies went into the promised land. Back to the land where they had stood on the edge. The spies reported, "Truly the LORD has given all the land into our hands. And also, all the inhabitants of the land melt away because of us" (Josh. 2:24).

Does anyone else feel like clapping your hands wildly here? They moved from fear to faith. They spied out the land and believed in the God who was calling them to go into that very land. Seeing through eyes of faith allowed them all to continue the journey of their brave steps of faith.

CLEAR VISION

The people-pleaser in me has a hard time at the eye doctor. Come with me here for a second.

I am blind as a bat without my contacts or glasses. Raise your hand with me if you understand the panic of not being able to find your glasses in the morning because they have fallen off the table, and you live alone and are on your hands and knees trying to feel around for them. At the eye doctor, they place this contraption thingy (the highly technical terminology for you here) in front of your eyes, and the eye doctor asks you to read the eye chart. Then comes the part the people-pleaser in me hates.

He flips from one lens to the next and says, "better or best."

Flipping back and forth, he wants me to say which lens helps me see more clearly. I know the answer is crucial because it will change my prescription—and well, let's be honest; seeing is an important thing.

I can tell he has an answer in mind, but it starts to get fuzzy. I am trying to read in his voice what he thinks I should say, what his opinion is of which lens I should see more clearly through. I need to stop myself from saying, "What do you want me to say?"

What if God were sitting in that eye-doctor chair and asking me the difference between what I saw with the lens of fear and the lens of faith? I would want to sign up right away for the supernatural prescription of faith. But why did I find myself feeling it more natural to pick the fear lens?

I like to picture God moving the contraption away so that I could see Him. Look into His eyes. Let Him see mine. Let Him see the way I see the land. Then watching His hands prescribe for me Psalm 34:4–10.

> *I sought the* LORD, *and he answered me*
> *and delivered me from all my fears.*
> *Those who look to him are radiant,*
> *and their faces shall never be ashamed.*
> *This poor man cried, and the* LORD *heard him*
> *and saved him out of all his troubles.*
> *The angel of the* LORD *encamps*
> *around those who fear him, and delivers them.*
> *Oh, taste and see that the* LORD *is good!*
> *Blessed is the man who takes refuge in him!*
> *Oh, fear the* LORD, *you his saints,*
> *for those who fear him have no lack!*
> *The young lions suffer want and hunger;*
> *but those who seek the* LORD *lack no good thing.*

A SCARLET THREAD OF HOPE

Tomorrow, my dearest friend in the world goes for infertility treatments. Receiving treatment is not her first time around this mountain. She has circled it many times before. My heart has broken with her as she has experienced negative pregnancy tests month after month. The pain of another loss through miscarriage or failed treatments feels like too much to bear.

If this is your story as you are reading these words, I want you to know that I am praying for you as I am typing. My heart is hurting for you. During my friend's journey, we have had many discussions about the burden of hope. Hope can be a terrifying thing. If we do not hope, we do not have to bear the weight and brokenness of disappointment.

Hope can feel like it is setting us up for a hard fall.

I told my friend that I want to continue to hold on to hope with her and for her when it may feel too hard and scary for her to hold it herself. I want these words to do the same for you.

Let me introduce you to a woman in Joshua 2. You may or may not have heard of her, but I think it is important to note that she makes the Jesus family genealogy in Matthew 1, so she is a pretty significant person. Rahab lived in the town of Jericho, and you'll remember that Joshua sent the spies to "Go, view the land, especially Jericho." They "came into the house of a prostitute whose name was Rahab and lodged there" (vv. 1–2).

Rahab may not have seemed like the likely choice for a model of faith. Her profession in town—a prostitute. The people of the city heard that there were spies in town, and they came looking at Rahab's house. Rahab took a bold step of faith by hiding the men. She told the spies that she had heard of the God of Israel. She had some bold faith in a God who was unfamiliar. "I know that the LORD has given you the land," she told the spies, adding, "and that the fear of you has fallen upon us, and that all the inhabitants of the land melt away before you" (Josh. 2:9). She reviewed for the spies what she and all of Jericho had already heard: of the drying up of the Red Sea and how they defeated the kings of the Amorites. In other words, they knew the Israelites were on the march.

As a result, "our hearts melted, and there was no spirit left in any man because of you, for the LORD your God, he is God in the heavens above and on the earth beneath" (v. 11).

There was some fear in that faith. She moved from that fear stop and took a shaky faith step when she stepped out in faith and made a request.

> *"Now then, please swear to me by the LORD that, as I have dealt kindly with you, you also will deal kindly with my father's house, and give me a sure sign that you will save alive my father and mother, my brothers and sisters, and all who belong to them, and deliver our lives from death." (vv. 12–13)*

I love that she asked for a sure sign. I think we go through those moments when we are in desperate need of a sign of hope. When I want a sign of hope, I want it to be *big*. Big enough that I can cling to it and know for sure that my life can depend on it.

As previously mentioned, I loved my camp counseling days. During one of my stints as a camp counselor, we were supposed to do the rock climbing/rappelling activity. I'll be honest; hand-eye coordination is not always my best game. Climbing attached to what felt like a way too small string up way smaller rocks, I would not be winning any Olympic competition here. It didn't help that when I get nervous, I laugh uncontrollably—and I was super nervous. When I laugh uncontrollably, I also have a hard time controlling other bodily functions (trying to be discreet here), so the whole thing could be—well, a disaster.

Then, there was the rappelling part. As the counselor, I was to be in charge at the bottom holding the rope: staying grounded and belaying (that's the fancy word for having a person's life in your hands by a string) the person who is hanging and coming down from the top. My holding a rope for someone else sounded like a terrible idea. Thin thread—a lot of risk—and the person was leaning back, trusting in my strength. That can be what hope feels like at times. Thin thread. A great deal of risk. Me leaning back and trying to trust in God's strength.

One of our biggest fears in saying yes to God can be holding on to hope in the outcomes of God.

Rahab decided to hold on to hope on a scarlet thread. The spies instructed her to "tie this scarlet cord in the window through which you let us down, and you shall gather into your house your father and mother, your brothers, and all your father's household." But she and her family had a responsibility too: "If anyone goes out of the doors of your house into the street, his blood shall be on his own head, and we shall be guiltless." The spies would guarantee their safety if they stayed inside and as long as they did not reveal the plans of the Israelites. Rahab promised to follow instructions and said, "According to your words, so be it." Take a moment to read this interesting account in Joshua 2:18–21.

> Rahab trusted her life and the life of her family to a scarlet thread of hope. What is your scarlet thread of hope?

It is comforting to me that Rahab asked for a sure sign. I think God put that in there to remind us that He knows that there are times we will find ourselves desperate for hope and need an assurance of the One we are hoping in. I can see myself trying to lean back on the wrong rope of hope, hoping that it will carry the weight of me.

THAT ONE TIME I CRASHED A SEGWAY

My friends recently took me on a trip to Washington, DC. They decided it would be the most fun thing in the world for us to take a Segway tour through downtown Washington to see the sights this way. If you are not familiar with a Segway, think of a circus unicycle except with two wheels and a motor. So maybe not like a unicycle at all now that I think about it! Can we take a second and remember my hand-eye coordination issues?

I knew this was going to be an unforgettable experience for me, for my group, and quite possibly for the Segway tour company. I was sure that was why they have safety video training and signed informed consent that riders will not sue the company. The first thing I noticed was that our tour guide was quite handsome.

The second thing I noticed was the safety videos about how you could crash your Segway were quite graphic and that I was glad they used stick figures instead of real people because I could see myself being the one crashing. In this small room with about fifteen other riders, they gave us directions about all things Segway. How to balance. How to turn. And most important, how to stop.

The unfortunate thing about all of this is there are no handlebars or brakes. You are the brakes and the handlebars. You turn your body to turn. You lean forward to go. And when you need to stop, you lean back. Nick, our cute tour guide, made us practice inside to prove we could function on the outside—in the real world. The real world where there was *real* traffic, *real* people, *real* small children and sidewalks and tourists and police around the White House.

He would speak into the headphones we were given to know how to follow his instructions, look out for obstacles, slow down, or turn. He also would be giving us random facts about Washington along the way, but I will tell you I didn't hear any of that because I was far too focused on not killing myself or anyone along the way with my Segway. I did like to pretend handsome Nick was whispering sweet nothings in my ear just for me—however, it was the whole group that he told to slow down for the approaching speed bump.

Things were going fine—until they weren't!

We hit that first downhill/slight turn/avoid the people, the traffic barrier, and the traffic, and I went blank. Even though Nick's voice was in my ear, I couldn't remember how to slow down for the life of me. I couldn't remember that I needed to trust and lean back.

So, I jumped. Off. The Segway.

It ran over me, or I ran over it, I am not sure. And the thing is, a Segway keeps going. Until Nick captured it. The whole group had to stop while I brushed myself off. My legs were shaking; I wanted to quit. I was embarrassed. I was slightly hurt. And I was terrified to keep Segway-ing through the city.

Nick asked me what part I was having a hard time understanding. "All of it!"

He reminded me, lean your weight back.

LEAN BACK

I can find myself having a hard time leaning my weight back on hope. I want to control hope. I want to control my expectations so I can control the outcome or control the disappointments. But when I lean back and risk hope in the character and compassion of God, He can bear the weight of me.

Rahab trusted her life and the life of her family to a scarlet thread of hope. What is your scarlet thread of hope? Don't just give the church answer here. What can you find yourself putting your hope in when you are not placing it in the One we can lean back on?

Is it hope in a wedding ring and the man of your dreams? Hope in your children's behavior? That they will turn out to be fine upstanding citizens who love God, make their beds, and make a difference in the world?

Hope in your job performance and that you will finally hear your supervisor say, "Job well done"? Hope in good grades? Hope in that friendship? Hope that this small group experience will turn out differently this time, and you will finally find your people? None of these things are bad things. They just aren't meant to be our hope-holder things.

> I do not want to be afraid to hold hope. Hope in the character, compassion, and promises of a God who is leading me to my promised land.

I do not want to be afraid to hold hope. To lean back on hope. To trust my life to hope. Hope in the character, compassion, and promises of a God who is leading me to my promised land. Even when it seems like just a scarlet thread.

Today, I am committing to letting go of the hope thread that tells me if people like me and think I am doing an excellent job in ministry that I am successful. I am grabbing on to the rope of hope that God sees me, designed me, and has a plan to use me for His glory in my story.

What about you? What is your scarlet thread of hope?

BACK TO RAHAB

Let's rejoin Rahab. In Joshua 6, we find the story of the fall of Jericho. The town where Rahab lived. Remember, she had put out the scarlet rope of hope as instructed. She moved from fear to faith as she hid the spies and asked for deliverance from destruction.

"Shout!" the commander Joshua ordered.

> *"For the LORD has given you the city. . . . Only Rahab the prostitute and all who are with her in her house shall live, because she hid the messengers whom we sent." . . .*
>
> *But to the two men who had spied out the land, Joshua said, "Go into the prostitute's house and bring out from there the woman and all who belong to her, as you swore to her." So the young men who had been spies went in and brought out Rahab and her father and mother and brothers and all who belonged to her. And they brought all her relatives and put them outside the camp of Israel. (Josh. 6:16–17, 22–23)*

The one who held on to that scarlet thread of hope ended up being in the lineage of Jesus—the One whose scarlet drops of blood dripped from the cross as our lifeline of hope.

MY YES PRAYER

Father, thank You for the example of Rahab, who had faith in a God she did not even know yet. Thank You that You gave her a scarlet thread of hope. I admit that hope is hard. Hope can be scary because it can lead us with a fear of disappointment. I confess that I can place my hope in the wrong things and hold on to hoping in threads that will not carry the weight of me. Help me find the faith to hope in You. In Your character. In Your faithfulness. In Your forgiveness and salvation. Help me to hold to the scarlet thread of hope in Jesus. In Jesus' name, Amen.

HEART WORK

Read Numbers 13; Joshua 2; Psalm 34:4–10; Hebrews 6:13–19.

What is God speaking to your heart as you read?

What is one fear stop currently on your heart?

What faith step will you pray about taking?

3

Rafts, Rivers, and Priests

I WANT TO LOVE WHITEWATER RAFTING. I live close to some of the best rapids in the country. I want to be all into the adventure. Then, I remember as a kid going tubing down a river that was not supposed to have large rapids. They left out the small fact that they were generating whitewater that day, and the rapids grew stronger as the water rose quickly. I got sucked into a whirlpool, which took off my shoes and other vital parts of my bathing attire that day.

This is not my favorite water flashback.

Because of my fear-of-missing-out personality, I have made myself go whitewater rafting a few times. Well, twice, to be exact. You should have seen me. The raft and I were one. I stuck my feet so tightly up against the side of that raft that there was *no* way that I was getting kicked out of the safety of that raft into the rolling water. There were those in my raft who wanted to "fall out" and find themselves in the rolling rapids.

I was not raising my hand for that one.

I did not know that they were taking pictures of me as we rafted, and I am going to tell you that the look on my face, a combination of horror and I-might-die-here-in-this-raft, was not my best look. There was no fake smiling here. I wonder how I would do if I were with the Israelites that day. That day when they knew there was a big obstacle between them and the promised land.

The Jordan River—no raft included.

Sure, they had heard stories of how God had done it before—how He had parted the Red Sea for their parents' generation, those who had fled Egypt under Moses' leadership. When they were being pursued by the Egyptians, God parted the Red Sea so they could pass through on dry land. The Egyptians chasing them did not fare so well. (You can read about it in Exodus 14.)

But this was not the Red Sea that the Israelites were now seeing right before their eyes: it was the Jordan River. Things feel different when you are looking at your own obstacle. Are you the type who sees an obstacle and wants to be the one who steps out in faith first? Or would you prefer to follow after others who have seen the barrier moved? Faith steps always involve those shaky first steps.

THE PRIESTS

I think it is noteworthy that in Joshua 3, the priests were to be the ones to take the first steps from fear to faith into the Jordan River. What do you picture when you think of the word *priest*? I imagine a clergyman with a collar. Or I picture the time I needed a cheap vacation, and I found out that you could stay at a monastery for free.

I found one in South Carolina near the beach and convinced my sister and a friend to join me there. We decided to follow most of the schedules of the monks who were there. We would spend our days in silence, walking the grounds, praying, studying the Word—and then at night, we would hang out and have a good old-fashioned sleepover in our cabin with lots of laughter, junk food, and games.

My first encounter with one of the priests there occurred when we first got to the monastery. The monastery had monks living there and guest priests who came to meet with retreatants who desired spiritual direction.

We arrived later in the evening, just as they were finishing their evening prayers. There is nothing quite as beautiful as hearing them sing through the Psalms, their mellow voices ringing through the stone walls in such a powerful way. We slid into our seats and listened with awe. Then came the time to exit.

It was a very dimly lit room. The monks and priests exited their stalls first, and then we, the visitors, were to leave next. There were about ten of us visitors who were there to spend a week at the abbey. I was not expecting as we exited the dimly lit room for the priest to splash holy water on our forehead as we left. Splash may be a bit dramatic of a word, but in the shadowy room, it felt like a splash of a surprise to me.

> One of the fears that can hold us back from saying yes to God is wondering, Do I matter to Him? Am I significant enough?

I let out a surprised scream. And then a laugh—the uncontrollable kind. You could hear both echoes through the walls of the hall. Here is a side note you should know about me in case we are not friends yet. I do not have a quiet, very proper, barely-there giggle. When I was in college, I had sinus surgery, and ever since then, when I laugh, loud snorts come out through my nose along with the laugh. Who knew that would be a surgery bonus prize. This was not in the informed consent.

The monks take a vow of silence from the end of evening prayers until mid-afternoon the next day, so they could not react. Can you imagine what was going through their heads as they tried to stifle any response to the hysterical laughter? I am surprised they did not kick us out of the monastery right then and there. They let us stay, and we had a delightful week.

The truth is, the priests for the Israelites had an essential job. God chose them to represent God's presence to the people. The key word here: chosen.

One of the fears that can hold us back from saying yes to God is wondering, Do I matter to Him? Am I significant enough?

I have to fight back the fears that come from lies that can sound loud, like a screamy laughter fit in a quiet monastery.

Do I matter to God?

Is God picking me to do THIS?

What if I succeed? What if I fail?

I have to remind myself that God calls me a priest. He calls you a priest. And that does not mean we must spend our days in a monastery. (Although I have to tell you, the food there is amazing. However, there is nothing stranger than eating a meal across from someone in silence.)

> *But you are a chosen race, a royal priesthood, a holy nation, a people for his own possession, that you may proclaim the excellencies of him who called you out of darkness into his marvelous light. (1 Peter 2:9)*

Chosen. Chosen by God to reflect the presence of God to people. Have you ever felt anything but chosen? Looked over? Unnoticed? Shrinking back in the background?

I love this quote from Heather Holleman in *Chosen for Christ*:

> Living a chosen life sets us free from the need to find validation anywhere else but in God—even when everyone else gains attention or awards. We don't need anyone else or any

experience to make us feel special or valued. And we're set free to settle into our lives because we believe God chose us for the life we're living.

And now, we take the first step into this chosen life.[4] (emphasis added)

It was a hefty calling to be a priest. If you don't skip over the book of Leviticus (let's be honest, that is the reason that keeps many of us from completing a read-the-Bible-in-a-year program), you see all the rules that went with being a priest because it was a high calling. When we place our yes on the table before the Lord, we are surrendering to our calling.

We can say that we are surrendering to His calling.

Let me pause here and say a calling does not mean that you have to be in vocational ministry. Your yes on the table to live as His chosen priest can be living an obedient yes to the adventure of motherhood, single life, starting a relationship, working at the grocery store, being a nurse, a CEO, or a Starbucks barista. Can we get an amen for the fact that you *are* a priest?

> A calling does not mean that you have to be in vocational ministry. Placing my yes on the table means stepping in instead of stepping away. Stepping into my calling to be His priest.

In accepting the invitation to be a priest, we recognize that we are HIS, and we live out His invitation to carry the people into the presence of God.

First Peter 2:9 tells me that I am a *royal* priesthood. Chosen with a calling to proclaim the excellencies of Him who called me out of darkness into the marvelous light. Sometimes fear/the world/my sense of laziness can convince me that it would be easier to let go of my "royal position" because it can seem like too much work. I can want to step away from these royal duties. Blend in. Do what feels natural versus stepping into the supernatural.

Placing my yes on the table means stepping in instead of stepping away. Stepping into my calling to be His priest. And recognizing that being His priest sometimes means being the one who takes the steps of faith first.

On my podcast *Coming Alive Conversations*, I get to interview the most amazing people who have placed their yes on the table before God. They tell the stories of how they sensed a calling from God. To write that book. To tell that story from the stage. To go to that place. To start that business. To be a stay-at-home mom.

In Episode 12 of Season 4, I interviewed Terrica Joy Smith. Her yes on the table led to starting the beautiful magazine *Eden and Vine*. She sensed God calling her to create this magazine but wondered how she could add this to the mix of her life.

> I came to the point where it was almost too difficult not to do it than to do it no matter how big it felt. The Lord called me to bring my loaves and fish. He spoke to my heart—do not concern yourself with the outcome. Bring your meager offerings. I will make the miracles.[5]

What a powerful statement. *Bring your meager offerings. I will make the miracles.*

I think of my friends Hailey Johnston and Joanna Ivey. Hailey was a mom who loved to sew. She began to see a need for employing women in her community who were struggling with homelessness. Placing her yes on the table before the Lord meant taking the first steps of faith that became Project Free2Fly, which supports, sustains, and nurtures women, employing them, training them, and loving them well through teaching them to make beautiful earrings, bags, and more. Joanna had her own sewing business and took the steps of faith to join Hailey in what God was doing at Project Free2Fly.

When I interviewed Hailey and Joanna on *Coming Alive Conversations* it was amazing to hear them talk about those first steps of faith when they sensed God calling them to this mission. Hailey said,

> I had to stand with my hands open. God, how do you want this to look? I was sitting in the bedroom one night, wrestling. I couldn't see what was coming. I didn't know what this would look like. I had fears what if we do not have the funds to support this? Then I realized you have to jump. Just do it.[6]

I loved hearing Joanna and Hailey talk about when Hailey sensed she needed to ask Joanna to come alongside and help her to accomplish this calling and dream. She knew they needed each other to see the dream grow. Joanna joined her creative business with Hailey's calling to Project Free2Fly, and God has done amazing things with their yes. I have loved watching one of their recent graduates of the program get her college degree, and now she is thriving in law school. I love following the stories of women getting their apartments after struggling with homelessness. Of women rescued from human trafficking. Of women being set free from a life of addiction. Hailey and Joanna are priests. (Priests that make the most beautiful accessories. I wear the earrings made in their program every day and get compliments wherever I go!)

Where are you in your story? What brave first step do you sense God is calling you to take? The answer to the where and the what will differ, but I imagine there is one thing that is the same across the board. There is some fear involved in putting that first foot in the water.

BACK TO THE BRINK

Let's go back to the brink of the Jordan River. If we could still see the footprints there, I would call them footprints of fear. When I see an obstacle, I can want to stop right there. Turn around. Go back to the safe. Take another route. Do anything that feels safer than that risk.

When I asked the question on social media: "I want to place my yes on the table before God, but I am afraid of _____," one of my close friends answered, "I am afraid of moving out of my comfort zone and trusting Him 100 percent with my future."

Another said, "What if I think I am saying yes to God, but I am heading down a path of destruction?"

Another, "I am afraid that I cannot trust the goodness of God because of the obstacles that I see."

On that trip to the Middle East, I not only visited Mount Nebo but also had the chance to visit the bank of the Jordan River, where it is believed the Israelites would have stood to cross over into the promised land. It was thought-provoking to stand on this side of the river bank. I had visited Israel before, so I had been on the other side looking over the Jordan into the country of Jordan. But this time, I found myself on the bank looking into the promised land.

Typically, the pilgrimage site of the Jordan River on the Jordan side is not very busy. Poor Jordan, they don't have quite the same touristic draw that Israel has—no Sea of Galilee, where you can ride a boat where Jesus walked on water. No tomb where you cannot find the risen Savior. No little town of Bethlehem or the site where Jesus may have been born. But they do have the Jordan River.

We had accidentally picked the Greek Orthodox day of Epiphany to visit the Jordan River. Epiphany is the day when they celebrate the baptism of Jesus by John the Baptist. As you can imagine, the Jordan River is a fine place to celebrate that day.

Thousands of people were there. Once you get your ticket (because, of course, for tourism's sake anywhere in the world, you pay a ticket price to see a thing), you got on a bus to be taken closer to the site. Then, you walked a path down to the waters. My friend, who had done this many times before, said on ordinary days hardly anyone would be on that path. Not this day. Our tour guide seemed a bit panicked. He kept telling us to keep up with him, and if we missed him to meet back at the bus at a specific time or he was leaving us. As much as I loved the idea of the Jordan River, I, for one, didn't want to be left, so I had to hold back from asking him if we could do it old-school kindergarten-field-trip-style where I hold on to his jacket with my friends making a line, each holding on to the one in front.

> What if God is calling you to be the one to go first?

Although trying not to get sucked into a massive crowd in this small path didn't seem to have the same sacred quiet experience I was expecting at the Jordan River, I am glad we went on that day. It made it easier to picture what it would have been like for the Israelites. It was a crowd. This large crowd gathered at the river bank. Then they waited for who would go first. Who would step their feet in the water? Then the crowd would follow.

What if God is calling you to be the one to go first?

If we stand on the riverbank together, I think these may be some of the fears we might be facing. Walking into a large body of a river—I would call that getting out of my comfort zone. I would call it having to trust Him 100 percent with my future in the promised land—because if He doesn't part this water, there will be no entering of the promised land.

I would wonder if this yes to God was leading to a path of

destruction by drowning. Take the time to read through this account, letting yourself hear Joshua's ringing words, stretch so you can see the priests going in first, smell the spray of the water as it rises, take your first steps in.

> *And as for you, command the priests who bear the ark of the covenant, "When you come to the brink of the waters of the Jordan, you shall stand still in the Jordan." And Joshua said to the people of Israel, "Come here and listen to the words of the LORD your God." And Joshua said, "Here is how you shall know that the living God is among you and that he will without fail drive out from before you the Canaanites, the Hittites, the Hivites, the Perizzites, the Girgashites, the Amorites, and the Jebusites. Behold, the ark of the covenant of the Lord of all the earth is passing over before you into the Jordan. Now therefore take twelve men from the tribes of Israel, from each tribe a man. And when the soles of the feet of the priests bearing the ark of the LORD, the Lord of all the earth, shall rest in the waters of the Jordan, the waters of the Jordan shall be cut off from flowing, and the waters coming down from above shall stand in one heap." (Josh. 3:8–13)*

A few times, while typing out this Scripture passage, I wanted to stop and shout glory. I refrained because I am on a writing retreat in a California cabin, and I didn't want to scare the people writing beside me. The water was overflowing its banks. But those priests. They took their step and stood firmly on dry ground.

GLOOOOOORRRRRYYYYYY!!!!!!!!!!!!

I pointed out that the priests were the ones to take the first steps. But what feels so freeing to me is that they were not the ones truly leading the charge. The ark of the covenant was. The ark represented the presence of God. I find this comforting. There are times when I have received the calling to take that first step of faith. To move from that fear stop to a faith step.

TAKING STEPS

Take a moment and think about what feels like your Jordan River right now. What obstacle do you see in the path in front of you? Where do you feel God drawing you to take a brave step of faith? Stand at the edge. Let's get cheesy here. Close your eyes. We no longer need the ark of the covenant to represent the presence of God because we have the presence of Jesus. Picture Him standing there in the middle of that water, beckoning you to come.

Peter had a moment like this. He was on the water. In a boat. While in the boat, he and the other disciples saw someone walking on water. They had the same reaction as I would. It's night. There are waves. I'm on a boat, and I see someone on the water! Am I on the scene of a horror film?

> *"It is a ghost!" and they cried out in fear. But immediately Jesus spoke to them, saying, "Take heart; it is I. Do not be afraid."*
> *And Peter answered him, "Lord, if it is you, command me to come to you on the water." He said, "Come." So Peter got out of the boat and walked on the water and came to Jesus. (Matt. 14:26–29)*

I wonder if Peter thought, "There is no way this is Jesus." Imagine his surprise when Jesus said, "Come!" I love that Peter did the thing.

He stepped out. He stepped in. He walked on water. I also love that he freaked out. He started to sink. I can find myself doing that as well. How about you?

I can step in the water in faith, and then fear overwhelms me, and faith quickly feels like sinking sand.

*But when he saw the wind, he was afraid, and beginning to
sink he cried out, "Lord, save me." Jesus immediately reached
out his hand and took hold of him, saying to him, "O you of
little faith, why did you doubt?" (v. 30)*

Jesus reached out His hand and took hold of him. The Israelite
people couldn't touch the ark of the covenant that represented the
presence of God. It was holy, and they were not. Peter could touch
the person of God. Jesus was holy, and Peter was not.

Jesus was the great High Priest, coming to represent the presence of God to the people. And today, when I picture myself on
that riverbank, the Jordan River, or the Sea of Galilee—I can
imagine Jesus standing in the water. He is beckoning me to take
those first faith steps and come. And when I feel like I am sinking,
He holds out His hand and takes hold of me.

He is beckoning you to take those first faith steps as you walk
out your yes to God. To come.

And when you feel like you are sinking, He is holding out His
hand and taking hold of you.

*But now thus says the LORD . . .
"Fear not, for I have redeemed you;
 I have called you by name, you are mine.
When you pass through the waters, I will be with you;
 and through the rivers, they shall not overwhelm you;
when you walk through fire you shall not be burned,
 and the flame shall not consume you.
For I am the LORD your God,
 the Holy One of Israel, your Savior." (Isa. 43:1–3)*

MY YES PRAYER

Jesus, I want to stand at the edge of this adventure of following You and say yes. I want to step my feet of faith into the water. But I admit I have some fear stops. Jesus, show me Your presence. Remind me of Your power. Open my heart and my eyes to see Your face and hear Your voice. To follow You. To trust that You will part the waters because You walk through them with me. I want to stand on the bank and say, sink or swim I am coming in!

HEART WORK

Read Joshua 3; 1 Peter 2:9; Matthew 14:22–33.

What is God speaking to your heart as you read?

What is one fear stop currently on your heart?

What faith step will you pray about taking?

4

Water-Crossing Miracles

I HAVE HAD A VARIETY OF CARS over the years that have kept me close to Jesus. I have done an earnest amount of praying that they would get me where I am going. It started with Toby the Taurus. Toby was a green Ford Taurus that I scored for a steal of a deal after I returned from the mission field. I loved Toby, but Toby did not always love me back.

There was a season when I had to pop the hood anytime I went anywhere and unhook Toby's battery so the battery wouldn't run down. Nothing says *I am here to be your professional speaker* like having to unhook your battery everywhere you go.

There was the one time when it was a freezing winter day, and I was wearing a scarf.

I leaned over the hood to unhook the battery, and there was a wind gush and a hood slam, and the scarf and I were stuck. Until my toothless upstairs neighbor came down in her nightgown to walk her poodle, and she popped the hood for me.

I knew the number of Toby's days was limited. I was driving on the interstate to a retreat, and I could not get Toby to go over 15 miles an hour uphill. Not the most ideal situation.

I will never forget the theme of that particular retreat. Blessed is she who believed.

I had a strongly worded prayer conversation with the Lord. *I want to believe. I want to trust that You are taking care of me. But You know that one of the only things I cannot do without is a car. I do not live in New York, God. I live in Tennessee. Without public transportation. And God, You know that I use Toby the Taurus to travel all over the United States for speaking engagements. I want to believe here, God, but I need a car that will go over 15 miles an hour.*

It was the *I believe, help my unbelief* type prayer.

Toby and I limped home from the retreat, and he died in my driveway.

I want to believe Lord—but I am experiencing some unbelief. You know I have given my life to serve You, right?

A few hours later, I had a friend call me and tell me that she needed to talk. Nothing strikes more fear in my heart than those words. I immediately begin thinking, *What did I do?*

I told her to come right over. We had just gotten settled when, a few minutes later, someone knocked on my door. It was some other friends of mine.

I will be honest, I was exhausted from the retreat, and maybe not feeling so hospitable. But I welcomed my friends to come in.

We had some initial chitchat, and then they said, "Jenn, we wanted to give you something."

I will never forget it. They handed me the keys and the title to a Honda Odyssey minivan. I was now the proud owner of a minivan. I called myself the soccer non-mom, and I *loved* it.

Blessed is she who didn't even believe and did see a fulfillment of a promise from the Lord.

THE RED SEA

Let's go back to when the Israelites left Egypt. This is the first generation who left, the generation who, due to their complaining and disobedience, was not allowed to enter the promised land. (It was their children's generation under Joshua's leadership who crossed the Jordan into the promised land.) You'll remember that after they fled from the Egyptians, God led them on what may not have seemed like the most direct path toward their promised land.

> *When Pharaoh let the people go, God did not lead them by way of the land of the Philistines, although that was near. For God said, "Lest the people change their minds when they see war and return to Egypt." But God led the people around by the way of the wilderness toward the Red Sea. And the people of Israel went up out of the land of Egypt equipped for battle. (Ex. 13:17–18)*

Sometimes, when I say yes to God, I can have some expectations for Him. I expect the most direct path to the promise. I can want quick, not slow. I can desire near, not far.

But God. God knows our hearts. He knew their hearts. He knew their fears might tempt them to want to return to the comfort of Egypt. Proverbs 3:5–6 is such a powerful reminder for me in those moments when I want to take the quick path to the promise, or I want to take the near when God's direction feels like the far.

> *Trust in the LORD with all your heart,*
> *and do not lean on your own understanding.*
> *In all your ways acknowledge him,*
> *and he will make straight your paths.*

I imagine when the Israelites saw the Red Sea coming, they had some questions for the pillar of cloud by day and pillar of fire by night that they were following. In chapter 14 of Exodus, the questions turned into groanings.

They saw a sea before them and the Egyptians marching up behind them. In their groaning, they pointed out that they felt like it would have been better for them to be in slavery in Egypt than to die in the wilderness. The Israelites were feeling raw emotions at this point. The faith steps were quickly becoming fear stops. "Fear not, stand firm," Moses tells them, "and see the salvation of the LORD, which he will work for you today. For the Egyptians whom you see today, you shall never see again. The LORD will fight for you, and you have only to be silent" (vv. 13–14).

> Sometimes, if we have grown up hearing the Bible's stories, we can forget the power of the Bible's miracles.

These words come filled with such power. I want to shout glory when I read the promise, "The LORD will fight for you, and you have only to be silent."

Get ready. You are about to see a miracle. Sometimes, if we have grown up hearing the Bible's stories, we can forget the power of the Bible's miracles.

Would you close your eyes (after you read these sentences, of course) and picture it with me? You are standing in front of a giant body of water that feels like it will swallow you whole. You look behind you and hear the sound of the Egyptians coming after you who will capture you and take you back to captivity.

You watch your leader Moses hold out his hand. You watch and wait. Your mind thinks through all the possible scenarios. Your knees may be trembling. You may grab the hand of your loved one next to you.

Will God be faithful to His Word?

*Then Moses stretched out his hand over the sea, and the L*ORD *drove the sea back by a strong east wind all night and made the sea dry land, and the waters were divided. And the people of Israel went into the midst of the sea on dry ground, the waters being a wall to them on their right hand and on their left. (Ex. 14:21–22)*

It happened. The water parted, and the people crossed the largest obstacle they had seen to their freedom journey to the promises of God. "Israel saw the great power that the LORD used against the Egyptians, so the people feared the LORD, and they believed in the LORD and in his servant Moses" (v. 31).

They saw the incredible power of the Lord, and so they believed. Until they got to the next obstacle and forgot again. I can find myself wanting to judge them when they forget what God has done. It was only one chapter over before the Israelites were groaning in fear again. The people in Exodus 15 sing right along with Moses all about what God had done, praising Him for His majesty, power, and glorious wonders. That was in verses 1–21.

Then there is a turn. Verse 22 finds them in the wilderness up against a different water problem—the bitter waters at Marah. The people grumbled *again*. They needed water, and what if the God they had seen part the water would not come through and give them drinkable water?

Different water obstacle, same miracle-working God.

OPAL THE ODYSSEY

I mentioned that I could find myself wanting to judge the Israelite people when I think about their quick unbelief. However, when I pause and examine my own heart and life, I realize I can be just like them.

See an obstacle, become afraid, and forget what God has done before.

I introduced you to my dear minivan Opal the Odyssey. I had the most fun being a minivan non-mom. Opal the Honda Odyssey and I drove all over doing speaking engagements and ministry events. You can get so much stuff into a minivan. Just as what happened when I was driving Toby the Taurus home from a speaking engagement and he broke down, I was on the way home from an event when Opal began "hiccupping."

They started as tiny hiccups. I remember grabbing my purple steering wheel cover that I had purchased from Goodwill and praying. I probably also turned the radio up because that's what I do when I want to pretend that the problem isn't happening.

Opal and I tried to make it up the hill but she ended up coughing, sputtering, and having to be pulled over to the side of the road before she turned off altogether.

I knew this was not good.

It just so happened that I was in an area of town where I knew someone who owned an auto repair shop, so I called him and had Opal towed away. I will never forget the moment when he called me a few hours later. I was with my friend who had picked me up. We were in the pharmacy getting a prescription she needed when the phone rang. The mechanic said, "Do you want the bad news or the bad news?"

> I wrote down the price he told me. A price that there was *no* way that I could pay.

I grabbed a notepad from the pharmacist, so I could take notes on what he said.

I still have that piece of paper I had when he told me that Opal needed a whole new transmission, and where I wrote down the price he told me.

A price that there was *no* way that I could pay.

I wrote down the amount and broke down into sobs. I am not typically a crying type, but here I was at the pharmacy counter, crying my eyes out.

That number on that piece of paper was impossible.

Didn't God remember? Didn't He know? Here I needed a miracle, and I forgot how I had seen God do one when I was in this very same situation before.

AT THE JORDAN RIVER

I wonder how the Israelites felt when they looked at the Jordan River. They had heard of the Red Sea parting for their parents' generation, but they had not experienced anything like it themselves. Stepping into the water took some faith steps. Some trust in the God who had provided manna in their wilderness wanderings.

As we studied in Joshua chapter 3, they did it. The priests went first, carrying the ark of the presence of God, and the rest followed.

On dry ground.

Then the Lord gave Joshua a rather interesting assignment. He was to pick one man from each of the twelve tribes and go back across the river.

They had already come through the obstacle, and God calls twelve men to go back—to go back into the water right there in the middle of it and grab a memorial stone.

I wonder if they had a hard time finding volunteers to want to go back into that water.

The Lord knew they needed a reminder. Something for them to look upon and remember the faithfulness of God.

> *When your children ask in time to come, "What do those stones mean to you?" then you shall tell them that the waters*

of the Jordan were cut off before the ark of the covenant of the LORD. When it passed over the Jordan, the waters of the Jordan were cut off. So these stones shall be to the people of Israel a memorial forever. (Josh. 4:6–7)

I was at my own Jordan River when I took the call at the pharmacy that day. I wish I had looked at the Honda Odyssey car keys as memorial stones and remembered the faithful provision of God in my past before I burst into tears and assumed I could not trust God with my present.

He is so faithful. He met me even in my forgetfulness and unbelief.

My friend Catrina decided to take me to dinner that night to cheer me up. While we were out, a mutual friend called and asked us to come over when we left the restaurant. So we did.

Catrina and I sat in their living room for a while. Our friend started getting a little teary-eyed. He said, "Jenn, God has told us to give you this."

They handed me the title and keys to their Toyota Camry.

What about the faithfulness of God!

By the way, I named the car after Catrina because she had been with me both times I was given a car, so it just seemed right.

I kept the scratch piece of paper that I had written the amount needed for a new transmission for Opal the Odyssey as a stone of remembrance.

I am currently looking outside my front window and can see Catrina the Camry parked outside. With over 200,000 miles on her, she is still getting me around. A stone of remembrance.

MORE THAN LUNCH

In Mark chapter 6, we find a crowd. Jesus tended to draw the multitudes. This crowd was large, and as the day went on, the people were hungry. Jesus' disciples suggested it was time to send them off to find some supper. "This is a desolate place," they pointed out, "and the hour is now late. Send them away to go into the surrounding countryside and villages and buy themselves something to eat" (Mark 6:35–36).

> In the hands of Jesus, He takes our little, and He can do much.

Hungry folks without a dollar-menu McDonald's anywhere.

Jesus handles the problem by asking the disciples what resources they have.

They point out the little they had. We have five loaves of bread and two fish.

In the hands of Jesus, He takes our little, and He can do much.

He took the five loaves and two fish, broke the loaves, blessed them, and then gave it to the disciples to distribute to the hungry among them.

They all ate and were satisfied, and there were twelve baskets of leftovers.

When God takes little and does much, there is more.

You may find yourself wanting to say yes to God, but wondering if you can trust the provision of God. (Remember me and my struggles of faith with my car situation as I raise my hand here.) The disciples saw God provide here in Mark 6 just what they needed in order to minister at that moment. Hop over to Mark 8, and they were in a crowd again.

A hungry crowd. You would think the disciples would remember that they had just seen Jesus feed five thousand. This crowd was even smaller by a thousand people. The disciples seem to have forgotten what had happened before. Jesus mentioned that the people had been with Him for three days and by now would be hungry. "And his disciples answered him, 'How can one feed these people with bread here in this desolate place?' And he asked them, 'How many loaves do you have?' They said, 'Seven'" (Mark 8:4–5).

Too bad the disciples had not saved a piece of the bread from before to remember that God could do it again.

Just like the Israelite people, the disciples tended to forget. Just like the disciples, we tend to forget. That is why we need to take up memorial stones.

Looking back at how God has worked in the past can help us with our plaguing fears in the present.

The same God of our yesterdays is working in our today, and He does not change.

SALVATION STONE

I can still remember the smell of the rose-scented diary pages. When I was a young girl I thought it was the coolest thing. Not only were the pages scented, but there was also a lock and key. A place for my seven-year-old self to lock away all my secrets. I am sure I wrote about how I sweet-talked my nice twin sister Michelle into making my bed. I was, after all, the older by one minute. (Can you believe that worked?)

In between going to vacation Bible school and church, I had heard about Jesus. I will never forget learning about heaven and realizing that I wanted to go there. I wanted to know Jesus, the one I read about in my Bible.

Naturally, I wanted to write about this desire to come to begin a relationship with Jesus in my rose-scented diary. However, I did not lock it away with the key. I wrote in the pages that I wanted to know how to *know* Jesus, ripped the page out of the diary, and my sister and I put our diary pages on our parents' bed.

Our parents were thrilled to find that ripped-off page. I remember the night so well. Our pastor's wife came over and talked with us, making sure our seven-year-old hearts understood how Jesus offered a relationship with Him and what accepting His gift of eternal life means. She led us in prayer, and I knew. I knew that night in my parents' living room that Jesus had just become my best friend. I knew that He loved me and had died on the cross for me and promised eternal life for me.

I love that my twin sister and I got to do it together with our parents there as we prayed.

I think it is vital that we take up the memorial stone of remembrance of our salvation stories. Taking this memorial stone of remembrance can help replace fear with the reminder of our faith's rescue story.

How did you come to know Jesus? Saying yes to Jesus' death, burial, and resurrection is the ultimate yes we place on the table. As John 3:16–17 assures us, "For God so loved the world, that he gave his only Son, that whoever believes in him should not perish but have eternal life. For God did not send his Son into the world to condemn the world, but in order that the world might be saved through him."

And "if you confess with your mouth that Jesus is Lord and believe in your heart that God raised him from the dead, you will be saved" (Rom. 10:9).

Remembering that we can trust God with our future eternal life can help us trust Him with our every day here on earth life. Let's celebrate the memorial stone of our salvation together.

SHAME-ROLLED-AWAY MEMORIAL STONE

Let's pick up another stone along with our salvation stone of re-membrance. Let's grab a memorial stone that I am going to call the shame-rolled-away stone.

The enemy of our souls loves for us to stay stuck in shame. The burden of carrying shame weighs our heart down in such a way that it affects every aspect of our lives.

> **The Lord wanted to show that the old was being made new.**

Do you fear that shame of your past mistakes and bondage disqualify you from the promised land?

In Joshua 5, the Israelites have now come into the promised land. The first thing that God told the Israelite people to do may seem strange at first glance. Circumcision.

The Lord wanted to show that the old was being made new.

> *And the LORD said to Joshua, "Today I have rolled away the reproach of Egypt from you." And so the name of that place is called Gilgal to this day. (Josh. 5:9)*

In this passage, looking at the Hebrew words makes what God wanted to show the Israelite people come alive.

The reproach of Egypt. Egypt was where they lived enslaved. In bondage. Not walking in freedom.

The word reproach here in Hebrew: *ḥerpâ* meaning disgrace, shame; reviling, taunt.[7] The name Gilgal meant to roll away. The Lord wanted to give a physical demonstration of what He was doing in their spiritual lives. Rolling away their shame. I don't know about you, but this is another thing that makes me want to shout glory.

I will never forget walking the Via Dolorosa in Israel. In case you are not familiar, the Via Dolorosa is the route in the Old City of Jerusalem that scholars believe to be the route where Jesus carried the cross. Part of the Via Dolorosa takes you right through the middle of the bustling marketplace.

The sights and sounds and crowds are an assault on the senses. Stalls and stalls of spices, olives, trinkets, and toys. A man on the tour tried to talk to me about the expensive cost of cashews and did not notice the tears streaming down my face. Maybe he wondered why the price of cashews made me so emotional.

Tears flowed as I thought about Jesus carrying the cross down these streets.

People in the ancient marketplace would have lined the streets—people watching Him carry the cross of shame. Like a common criminal, the Savior of the world was mocked by the very people He had created to live in this world.

Then the soldiers of the governor took Jesus into the governor's headquarters, and they gathered the whole battalion before him. And they stripped him and put a scarlet robe on him, and twisting together a crown of thorns, they put it on his head and put a reed in his right hand. And kneeling before him, they mocked him, saying, "Hail, King of the Jews!" And they spit on him and took the reed and struck him on the head. And when they had mocked him, they stripped him of the robe and put his own clothes on him and led him away to crucify him. (Matt. 27:27–31)

While walking that road in Israel, I felt the Lord whisper. *I carried your shame, so you did not have to.*

Can you let that sink in, friends?

He carried our shame so that we do not have to. With nail prints in His hand, He took the old and made us new. Second

Corinthians 5:17 says, "Therefore, if anyone is in Christ, he is a new creation. The old has passed away; behold, the new has come."

The circumcision in Joshua represented that the old reproach of Egypt had been rolled away to the new in the freedom of the promised land.

Friend, if you are in Christ, you have been made new. It can be easy to get stuck in old patterns of sin and shame, especially in our brain's ways of fear and bondage.

Let Him roll away your reproach. Your past mistakes do not disqualify you from saying yes to all that God has for you.

MY YES PRAYER

Jesus, thank You that You carried the cross of shame so that I do not have to. You rolled away my reproach. Today, I celebrate that I am a new creation in Christ Jesus. Jesus, help me heal from any areas of shame that the enemy wants me to stay stuck. Help me walk out of patterns of bondage and slavery to sin. An area where I need to see You work is:

Please help me remember Your faithfulness in the past and that You are working here in my present. I want to take up stones of remembrance. In Jesus' name, Amen.

HEART WORK

Read Exodus 14; Joshua 4; Mark 6:30–44; Joshua 5:1–10.

What is God speaking to your heart as you read?

What is one fear stop currently on your heart?

What is a faith step you will pray about taking?

5

Manna in the Wilderness

I CONFESS. When the coronavirus pandemic started and there was a run on toilet paper, I was unsure what to think. I tend to be Polly Positive. I like to live in my happy everything-will-be-fine-and-this-will-go-away-in-a-few-weeks world. I didn't go out and buy any. I would be fine.

That is until I needed toilet paper. I scoured all the stores. I could have never imagined a shortage of the fundamental thing of a roll of paper that flushes down the toilet. You know it isn't good when even the one-ply generic, more like sandpaper, is gone. My sweet friend Catrina rescued me as usual. (She is the friend I named my car after.) She brought me some of those treasured rolls.

My mom's birthday was right around the time of the great toilet paper shortage of 2020. I could not have dreamed that for her birthday, I would find myself climbing on the bottom three shelves of the grocery store in the toilet paper aisle because there was one very last package of her favorite brand left, and it was hidden away at the very top. My sister snapped a picture before I and the golden toilet paper package came tumbling down. Any bodily harm was worth it for one of my mom's favorite birthday presents ever.

Around the same time of year, everyone started homesteading. You could not find yeast. People everywhere were making home-made bread. I don't even eat bread due to food allergies, but if everyone was doing it, I wanted to do it. If I couldn't find yeast, then I needed to figure out how to make my own.

I became one of "those people." The ones who had a sourdough starter and learned to make bread from it.

I had little to no faith in my ability to bake. I enjoy cooking because I can do it with my flair. I am a make-up-things-as-I-go kind of girl. Baking is much more of a science. Bread baking is a very prescriptive science that involves not only baking the bread but feeding the starter and keeping it alive.

I am proud and shocked to say a year later I still had a living starter to make bread from every week.

During the pandemic, people got desperate, thinking there would not be enough provisions for them. There was a great deal of stockpiling and gathering to make sure they had enough resources. This reminds me of the Israelite people. We find them desperate, not for toilet paper but for bread.

DESPERATE FOR BREAD

In Joshua 5:12, we read that the manna ceased the day after they ate of the land's produce. There was no longer manna for the peo-ple of Israel, but they ate of the fruit of the land of Canaan.

For that statement to mean anything to us, we need to remind ourselves what the story of manna was about. Maybe you grew up as a church girl like me, and this story has become very familiar to you. What if we study and read it as we have never heard it?

Let's take ourselves back to the desperate moments of 2020 when there was no toilet paper, yeast, or pasta sauce. What if you think about yourself on your knees begging God to provide because you are out of ideas how to provide for yourself?

Come with me to the book of Exodus, chapter 16. The Israelite people, under Moses' leadership, had left Egypt and come to the wilderness of Sin. It was the fifteenth day of the second month of their journey away from Egypt. Right about the time in a trip when the journey isn't so new and adventurous anymore. When you find yourself homesick for what you knew, even if what you experienced was slavery.

They were tired and hungry. I don't make the best decisions when tired and hungry. I can find myself looking frantically to see if I have any Little Debbies hidden anywhere and shoving my face with those yummy snack cakes until I want to pop, even though the ones I happened to find had expired five years before. The people said to Moses and Aaron,

> We start to dream about the "meat pots and bread" and forget about the promises found in the journey to our promised land.

"Would that we had died by the hand of the LORD in the land of Egypt, when we sat by the meat pots and ate bread to the full, for you have brought us out into this wilderness to kill this whole assembly with hunger." (Ex.16:3)

Truth be told, when we take the adventure of placing our yes on the table before God, we will have moments like this. Moments when the before our yes steps seem better than our unknown scary in the middle of the yes steps.

This can become a fear stop. I think it is grace for us to acknowledge this. To watch for this. Even though I like to be Polly

Positive, to expect this. We start to dream about the "meat pots and bread" and forget about the promises found in the journey to our promised land.

As a counselor, I have the blessing of sitting with someone longing to leave their Egypt. To move into freedom.

I have heard the heartbreaking stories of bondage. Of slavery to fear. Hard stories of trauma and wanting to break free from the lies that come with that trauma. Stories of addiction and longing to be free. Stories of a significant person in their life telling them all the ways they cannot or should not walk in their dream or calling. Stories of heartbreak and deep ache.

Many times they are holding a version of this question in their hearts. If I leave Egypt and place my yes before God, will He provide what I need for the journey? What if He doesn't?

The Israelites were at the point they were convinced He wouldn't provide.

I have had moments where I was convinced of that as well. In those moments in God's grace, He comes.

> *Then the LORD said to Moses, "Behold, I am about to rain bread from heaven for you, and the people shall go out and gather a day's portion every day, that I may test them, whether they will walk in my law or not. On the sixth day, when they prepare what they bring in, it will be twice as much as they gather daily." So Moses and Aaron said to all the people of Israel, "At evening you shall know that it was the LORD who brought you out of the land of Egypt, and in the morning you shall see the glory of the LORD, because he has heard your grumbling against the LORD. For what are we, that you grumble against us?" (vv. 4–7)*

This is what He did. He gave them bread in the wilderness even though it was a kind of provision they had never seen before. Some scholars say the Hebrew meaning of manna is "what is it."

God's provision may not always come in the way we expect or have seen before, but it comes.

MOLDY MANNA

I am someone who loves her coffee. I have coffee mugs everywhere. My car sometimes looks like a rolling coffee shop. Please tell me that I am not the only one who has this problem. All my to-go coffee mugs have no problem with the to-go part of getting in my car. But for some reason, I have trouble getting them back into the house from my vehicle.

They tend to pile up a bit. The cup-holders—full. The floorboards—full. The trunk, well, it has some as well. Maybe this is why I am still single. No Proverbs 31 woman status here. I am sure she didn't leave her coffee mugs in the pack of the donkey.

Yesterday I finally got up the nerve to make myself take the cups in and clean them out.

Here's a little tip for you. When there is a little liquid remaining in the back of the cup, mold tends to form. I think I may or may not have found several cures for cancer in my moldy mugs.

You wouldn't find me taking a big old swig of what remained in those mugs. If I needed a strong Americano (with cinnamon powder sprinkled on top), I would hop in the car and order a brand-new one.

The Israelites had a problem with mold as well. Their concern was moldy manna. The Lord gave specific instructions for them to gather what they needed for that day.

*This is what the L*ORD *has commanded: "Gather of it, each one of you, as much as he can eat. You shall each take an omer, according to the number of the persons that each of you has in his tent." And the people of Israel did so. They gathered, some more, some less. But when they measured it with an omer, whoever gathered much had nothing left over, and whoever gathered little had no lack. Each of them gathered as much as he could eat. (vv. 16–18)*

Promised the exact provision that they needed for that day. However, they were afraid. They didn't trust God with the provisions for the day, so they tried to leave parts of it until morning.

What they got instead of a yummy breakfast treat were maggots and mold. Verse 20 says, "But they did not listen to Moses. Some left part of it till the morning, and it bred worms and stank. And Moses was angry with them."

I can judge them until I think about myself. I think about how I can try to fight the fear of tomorrow by gathering more than I need for today.

> Jesus tells us not to be anxious about tomorrow, for tomorrow will be anxious for itself. Rest in His provision for today. Let's fight fear with the faith that God provides day by day.

It may not be in trying to stockpile financial resources. It may be in accumulating worries. As if collecting worse-case scenarios in my thoughts can provide the peace that I want.

It may be in stockpiling a sense of control and checking off my to-do list. Making sure everyone likes me all the time. Staying safe and unwilling to risk.

God tells us in Lamentations 3:22–23 that His mercies are new every morning.

Jesus tells us in Matthew 6:34 not to be "anxious about tomorrow, for tomorrow will be anxious for itself." Rest in His provision for today. In this same passage, Jesus reminds us that we do not have to worry about our lives. The same God who provides for the birds of the air and the lilies of the field is providing for us.

My big worry about having a ministry tends to be financial. I can find myself asking, will God continue to provide for this yes?

Your big worry might be something completely different. You may feel called to be a stay-at-home mom but worry what others will think. You may sense God calling you to serve on the mission field but don't know the where, how, or what God has in store.

You may be reading this and want to step out and share the gospel with your friend who doesn't know Jesus, but you worry you will not have the answers to their questions or the right words to say.

You may be reading this and wondering how you will ever be free from that secret addiction.

God will provide. It may look different than we expect. It may come at a different timing than we hope. But the giver of good gifts will give.

I am continuously amazed at the manna giver. Even as I was writing these words at a coffee shop, I got a notification ding on my watch. Someone had just made a donation to my ministry— unasked for and unexpected.

It made me smile so big at the loving timing of the Lord. I had just typed the words *my big worry having a ministry tends to be financial.* It was as if God winked, smiled, and said, "Let Me remind you that I give manna in the wilderness."

Friend, let's fight fear with the faith that God provides day by day.

It can be tempting to try to fight our fears of tomorrow by gathering more than we need today, but let's take a page from what the Israelite people learned. There is no need to eat moldy manna.

Hundreds of years later, Nehemiah added some interesting things to the history of this time: "You gave your good Spirit to instruct them and did not withhold your manna from their mouth and gave them water for their thirst. Forty years you sustained them in the wilderness, and they lacked nothing. Their clothes did not wear out and their feet did not swell" (Neh. 9:20–21).

I love the details Nehemiah gave us there. Their feet did not even swell. When I travel or hike, my feet do swell, so I think that was a reminder of the kindness in the character of God.

I had a specific name-brand type of sandals once. I wanted to love them because everyone talked about them as if they were the shoe Jesus Himself would have worn. Two straps went over my big toe. My big toe is well—big, so I always felt like it was cutting my circulation off.

I will never forget the time I traveled to Haiti. Between flying and the heat, my feet swelled. I couldn't get those sandals back on my feet. I may or may not have had to steal a pair of flip-flops we had brought for the orphan kids so that I could have shoes for the week.

THE FRUIT OF THE LAND

When the twelve spies were sent by Moses to check out the promised land, I find it interesting Moses instructed them to bring back a sample of the land's fruit. No touristy I WAS HERE mugs or magnets for them; they wanted to know how the fruit was. And it was tremendous!

In fact, when they got to the valley of Eschol and cut down a branch with grapes on it, they had to carry it on a pole between two of them. Let's say I have not seen grapes like that in my local grocery store, have you? Here's what they said: "We came to the land to which you sent us. It flows with milk and honey, and this is its fruit" (Num. 13:27).

So now in Joshua 5, we find the people of Israel of the next generation (remember, that due to complaining and disobedience, the original Israelites who left Egypt did not get to enter the promised land) all together and ready to celebrate the Feast of the Passover. Let's take a little refresher on the Passover. In Exodus 12 we are told all about the Passover. The Israelites had precise instructions from God Himself about how and when to celebrate this feast. He also told them continue to commemorate this occasion "throughout your generations" (Ex. 12:17).

What were they celebrating? That when the angel of death came for the firstborn in the land of Egypt, they would be passed over if they had been obedient and placed the blood of a lamb on their doorposts. The blood of the lamb rescued them.

Sound familiar? The blood of the lamb, Jesus, rescued *us*.

The Israelites were doing just as God instructed them. Celebrating the Passover, but this time in the land of promise. I feel like we should let that sink in. The generation before them had spent years of wandering in the wilderness. Years of not being in the place they left Egypt to come live. And here it is—celebration time for Joshua, Caleb, and the new generation.

> The manna ceased because the Lord knew they would keep trying to eat the manna and miss the fruit of the promise.

Let's join the celebration with them. Imagine what it must have felt like to be there—encamped at Gilgal together. The place whose name means to roll away as a reminder that the shame of Egypt had rolled away from them.

And the day after the Passover, on that very day, they ate of the produce of the land, unleavened cakes and parched grain. And the manna ceased the day after they ate of the produce of the land. And there was no longer manna for the people of Israel, but they ate of the fruit of the land of Canaan that year. (Josh. 5:11–12)

Finally! The fruit of the promised land, that luscious fruit Moses' spies had been so impressed with a generation ago.

I think the manna ceased because the Lord knew they would keep trying to eat the manna and miss the fruit of the promise.

I can do that. I can snuggle into my comfort zone, settling for what I think satisfies my soul, and miss the good gifts the Father has for me.

God always provides what we need. I don't want to miss that provision because I am stuck on how He provided in the past. My faith steps? Watch God provide and eat His excellent fruit.

The disciples almost missed Jesus' *new* provision for bread at their last Passover feast with Him. They were expecting the usual breaking and passing of bread and wine at the table, according to the rites of the Passover meal. But Jesus changed the menu. He told them they were eating not bread but His body.

Drinking not wine, but His blood.

Can you imagine how confused they were? This was not the feast they were accustomed to experiencing. This was not what they expected. The provision of Jesus' body was not what they were expecting when they passed the bread.

But He knew it was what they needed. When they gathered around the table for the traditional Passover meal, Jesus took bread and in those often-repeated ringing words said, "This is my body, which is given for you. Do this in remembrance of me." You can read about this in Luke 22:14–20.

Perhaps they even remembered what He had told them earlier in His ministry: "I am the living bread that came down from heaven. If anyone eats of this bread, he will live forever. And the bread that I will give for the life of the world is my flesh" (John 6:51).

Friend, how have you seen God provide? How are you watching for God to provide? What are your fears about His provision as you say yes to Him? Let's say a yes prayer together, reminding our hearts the Bread of Life satisfies the needs in our life.

MY YES PRAYER

Jesus, thank You that You are the Bread of Life. That Your body was broken for me, Your blood was shed for me. That You promise that if I hunger and thirst for You, I will be satisfied.

Jesus, I admit I get scared. I find myself afraid that You will not provide. I forget that You are my provider, and I wear my heart and mind out trying to figure it out all myself.

Right now I give You my worries about provision in:

Help me watch for You. To wait on You. To trust You.

Thank You for the ways You have provided in the past. Thank You for manna and the fruit of the land. Please help me not to be like the Israelites trying to keep moldy manna. Instead, please give me the faith to trust Your provision for each day. Here is my yes Lord.

In Jesus' name, Amen.

HEART WORK

Read Joshua 5:10–15; Exodus 16; Matthew 6:25–34.

What is God speaking to your heart as you read?

What is one fear stop currently on your heart?

What faith step will you pray about taking?

6

Behind the Walls

A LITTLE WARNING FOR YOU if you ever want to go on a trip overseas with me. I laugh about this, but it has tended to be true. Every time I am supposed to go on a ministry trip somewhere, the embassy puts out a travel warning to that country for some reason or another.

There is some rare new mosquito-borne illness, cholera outbreak, or political uprising, to name a few. Feel like signing up for me to lead your church's mission trip?

You might not want to put your yes on that table.

I had been to Haiti many times and had fallen in love with a particular remote city. Whenever I learned of a trip, I was all in to be there.

We packed our bags full of the supplies to do VBS for six hundred kids for that week (I cannot even describe to you the amount of happy chaos that is), supplies for the special needs camp, and gifts and supplies for the orphans and widows that we ministered to in this city. Here we go!

The airport is chaotic, so the chaos happening did not seem highly unusual to those of us who had been there many times. The same is true of the streets.

Our group and all our suitcases and supplies packed into the back of the tap-tap truck. I remember laughing and being so happy that we were there. We were joking and even singing, oblivious that there was any reason not to.

I did find it strange that we seemed to be circling the same area on the road and not continuing the way to our midpoint where we would stop for the night. But then again, I am terrible with directions in America, so I didn't expect to know where we were in Haiti.

I thought it odd when we stopped at a guesthouse so soon into our trip but did not expect what happened next. The tap-tap drivers told us to get out. They shut and locked the gates and told us we needed to harbor here in this guesthouse.

There had been a political uprising, and things were getting dangerous fast. The gravity of the situation hit us a few hours later when a van full of very shaken American women came through the gate.

These missionary women had gotten stuck on the roads in the middle of the uprising. Their car windows were broken out and one had been injured badly from the bricks thrown at the vehicle.

The gate was closed behind them, and our group found ourselves stuck behind these guesthouse walls. We quickly found out the airport was shut down, and we were the last plane that had been able to enter. CNN was broadcasting, the embassy was calling, advising us to shelter in place. Behind the walls.

We find a different scenario behind the walls in Joshua 6. You might remember from chapter 2 that the people of Jericho had heard about the strength of the coming Israelites so, "Jericho was shut up inside and outside because of the people of Israel. None went out, and none came in. And the LORD said to Joshua, 'See, I have given Jericho into your hand, with its king and mighty men of valor'" (Josh. 6:1–2).

In Haiti, we were finding safety behind the walls.

In Jericho, the citizens were holed up behind the walls. And the Israelite people needed God to tear down those thick walls.

The same God was working in both scenarios.

It was not our plan to come to Haiti and have to shelter in place behind walls. It was not in our schedule to see the burning tires right outside our gate from the riots. It was not our plan to play 5,672 rounds of Phase 10 with cards tinged with the floating ash coming from the fires. (I did not even win one of those 5,672 rounds of Phase 10.) It was not in our plan to have to pray through what to do.

After several days of sheltering in place behind the walls, we prayerfully decided for most of the team to make a

> We had our mission plan for the week, and God had His.

run for the city we had come to serve. It's a long journey, and there was lots of praying, but we made it. We got to the town, and it was 100 percent worth it to get to hug the widows, orphans, VBS kids, and special needs adults we had come to love.

One smile of one of our special needs teenagers—whose mom carried her over rocky, hilly terrain to bring her to our day of the camp—made it worth leaving from behind those walls.

We had our mission plan for the week, and God had His.

After one packed full day of ministry, we were on our way to visit one of the widows when we got the call. We needed to evacuate ASAP and get back to the central city and the airport to fly out. This would require an overnight evacuation complete with a hired SWAT team for our protection.

It was surreal. We prayed—*lots*. My church prayed—*lots*. An emergency overnight evacuation was not in our plans.

On that overnight evacuation back—about an eight-hour trip—I will say I had some fear. But I also had a sense that God wanted to remind us of His power. His presence. Of His promise in Psalm 91:1–2:

> *He who dwells in the shelter of the Most High*
> *will abide in the shadow of the Almighty.*
> *I will say to the LORD, "My refuge and my fortress,*
> *my God, in whom I trust."*

What did God teach me? That it was all worth it, even for a moment to see our special needs friends smile. To hug that widow. He taught me that sometimes we have to leave our walls that feel safe and press through to see what He wants to do.

I bet the Israelites had all kinds of ideas about how to get past the walls of Jericho. However, I imagine that they did not come up with the same plan that God had for them.

We have a God who takes what does not make sense in the natural and infuses it with His supernatural power and plan. We get to see the miraculous unfolding of His glory in our stories.

WALKING AROUND THE WALLS

Have you ever had the moment when you get stuck in fear because you wonder how the plan the Lord is giving you could be better than your plan because His plan doesn't even seem to make sense?

I am sure there were some mumblings and grumblings among the Israelite people about this very thing when they looked at the walls of Jericho.

They had all kinds of ideas of how to knock those walls down, but the plan the Lord gave them was not top of their ideas list.

> *You shall march around the city, all the men of war going*
> *around the city once. Thus shall you do for six days. Seven*

priests shall bear seven trumpets of rams' horns before the ark. On the seventh day you shall march around the city seven times, and the priests shall blow the trumpets. And when they make a long blast with the ram's horn, when you hear the sound of the trumpet, then all the people shall shout with a great shout, and the wall of the city will fall down flat. (Josh. 6:3–5)

I would not want to be on the team that marched around the city if we had to be quiet the whole time. "You shall not shout or make your voice heard," was Joshua's command, "until the day I tell you to shout. Then you shall shout" (v. 10).

I am awful at forced quiet. I find myself getting uncontrollable giggles, or I try to whisper to my friend next to me, and let's say I do not have the best whisper voice.

The plan to quietly walk around the walls until it was time to blow the trumpet loud and then the walls would come down would have seemed crazy to me.

I find it interesting that the Lord gave Joshua the promise before He gave Him the plan.

In Joshua 6:2, He promised Joshua that He had delivered Jericho into his hands. Then He tells him how they are going to see it happen.

When I asked people to complete the statement, "I want to say yes to God, but I am afraid of _____," many responded with their fears of what others would think of their faith steps. Another response that I repeatedly received was they were worried they would not hear God's plan correctly.

I wonder if the temptation was to stop marching because what in the world were the people thinking inside? Or if they doubted that Joshua had heard this plan correctly.

Would I have kept marching? Would you have?

For my thoughts are not your thoughts,
neither are your ways my ways, declares the LORD.
For as the heavens are higher than the earth,
so are my ways higher than your ways
and my thoughts than your thoughts. (Isa. 55:8–9)

On my first trip to Nepal, I went as a summer missionary. I was pursuing my master's in counseling and learned of a need for someone to work with a hospital social worker to provide counseling to patients. This sounded like a perfect plan to serve Jesus for the summer.

There were four of us on a team who met for the first time at training in India before we went to Nepal to begin our summer work.

Imagine our surprise when we got to Nepal, and things did not quite go according to our team's summer work plan. We were assigned to work at the hospital, but not in the ways that we had planned.

God often gives us His promises before His plan because He knows we may feel overwhelmed, confused, or frightened by the plan.

Our team leader guided us into the central sterile supply room. As we sat around a table, a translator explained our job for the summer.

In this tiny room, we would work with about five Nepalese women. We would be learning how to take cotton and gauze and make maxi pads for the maternity ward. This was our summer assignment. Maxi pad–making for Jesus.

Imagine trying to write home about that in your prayer newsletter.

I am not going to lie. I doubted this plan of God often that summer. Why in the world was this what He had sent me to do? But God's higher ways knew that making those maxis in that tiny room would be when God broke my heart for this nation and called me back there to serve.

How have you seen God call you to a plan that does not seem to make sense at the time? But as you say yes, have you seen that His ways and thoughts are higher than you could have dreamed or planned?

I think God often gives us His promises before His plan because He knows we may feel overwhelmed, confused, or frightened by the plan.

WHEN WE SAY YES

Every Sunday at my church, the Greenhouse, I sit in the high school auditorium in awe of God. I have had the joy of having a front-row seat to God's plans unfolding there. Literally. I sit there in the very front row with my sister.

I remember when my brother-in-law first brought up the idea of moving back to his tiny hometown of Athens, Tennessee, to plant this church. My sister was not quite feeling that calling. She told him, "I do not think God is calling us to Athens. We need to stay right where we are."

There came a turning in her heart when she knew God was asking her to surrender. To say yes. To move their family to Athens and begin the journey of starting this church.

She said yes to God as they moved to Athens without knowing where their family of five (at the time) would live or where Todd would find work. And now she says yes to God from the front row every Sunday. I may be biased, but she is the most incredible pastor's wife, often opening her home and heart to shepherd those God has brought to the Greenhouse Church.

Every baptism, every marriage saved, every sermon preached, every person set free from addiction, every international student who has heard and accepted the gospel for the first time reminds me of the power of God's plans versus ours. The power of yes.

Every Tuesday, I have the blessing of interviewing extraordinary Christian leaders on my podcast *Coming Alive Conversations*. It makes me giggle every time I sit down at the tall bistro-style table in my tiny one-bedroom apartment where I set my podcasting microphone up. Why do I laugh? Because I always forget the barstool is broken at the bottom and that I need to sit down delicately. Right before I remember, I usually end up on the floor.

Then I laugh because I am about to interview some of my faith heroes. Bestselling authors, those leading influential organizations changing the world, people I would never have imagined I would get to talk to from my small apartment.

I laugh when my neighbor interrupts an interview knocking loudly on the door to ask if I have a plunger. I laugh when the UPS man always seems to drop off the package I have been waiting for right at the interview time. And I laugh because of the goodness of God. I cannot believe I get to do this.

In each interview, I hear stories of God's plans intersecting the interviewee's surrendered yes to God. How they could not have imagined what God had in store. What my friend Cindy Bultema called a plot twist in her interview. Cindy shares how she was knee-deep in a speaking and writing ministry that she loved when she dreamed that she was the International GEMS Girls Club's executive director. She woke up from the dream, prayed, and sensed she was supposed to ask if they were looking for an executive director, and they were.[8]

Today as I type, this is her four-year anniversary to saying yes to leading a ministry that has great impact on the lives of over 25,000 girls every year worldwide.

What walls are you encountering right now? What looks impossible? What crazy plan do you sense the Holy Spirit whispering to your heart?

The Israelites obeyed the Lord's wild plan. They marched. And marched. And marched some more. Can you imagine the moment when it was the time to shout in victory? I wonder if they doubted they would see this victory.

But they did it. They marched and then shouted. The trumpet was blown.

> *So the people shouted, and the trumpets were blown. As soon as the people heard the sound of the trumpet, the people shouted a great shout, and the wall fell down flat, so that the people went up into the city, every man straight before him, and they captured the city. (Josh. 6:20)*

Friends, we serve a God of the impossible. Heaven coming to earth in the form of baby Jesus to virgin Mary—impossible made possible.

Jesus taking a few loaves of bread and fish and feeding 5,000—the impossible made possible.

A woman who had a bleeding disorder for years touching the hem of Jesus' garment and made well—the impossible made possible.

> May you be encouraged that the wall-knocking, food-multiplying, paralytic-and-disease-healing, giant-slaying God is still working in the impossible today.

The paralytic man picking up his mat and walking home—the impossible made possible.

Rahab letting out the scarlet rope and believing God to protect her and her family—the impossible made possible.

People walking around the thick walls of Jericho and the walls coming down—the impossible made possible.

Each of these stories involved instructions from God that may have seemed crazy when they heard them. Each of them had to take faith steps.

Today may you be encouraged that the wall-knocking, food-multiplying, paralytic-and-disease-healing, giant-slaying God is still working in the impossible today.

MY YES PRAYER

God, thank You that You are the God of the impossible made possible. That Your plans are much higher than my plans. I confess my fears in following these plans. I want to trust You but I confess my fear. Today I look at these walls:

Jesus, would You show me my next faith steps? Would You give me the courage to believe? Would You forgive me for wanting to do things my way? Thank You for your plans. Thank You for your faithfulness. I pray Proverbs 3:5–6 that You will help me trust in You with all my heart and not lean on my own understanding. In all my ways, may I acknowledge You and trust that You will make my paths straight.

HEART WORK

Read Joshua 6; Psalm 91; Proverbs 19:21; 1 Samuel 17; Luke 8:43–48.

What is God speaking to your heart as you read?

What is one fear stop currently on your heart?

What faith step will you pray about taking?

7

Victory
and Defeat

ARE YOU THE COMPETITIVE TYPE that likes to win? I don't
think I am until I get in a competition. Frankly, I was never good
at sports (that whole hand-eye coordination thing gets me every
time), but I can slay at some badminton. When my sister and I
get into a badminton competition—game on. I want the victory!

Victory. Even reading those words feels good. The Merriam-
Webster dictionary defines victory as "achievement of mastery or
success in a struggle or endeavor against odds or difficulties."[9]

I once felt so proud of myself for winning a prize in a 5K race,
first place of women in my age division. You would have thought
I was an Olympian instead of someone participating in a 5K
fundraising trail run. I was victorious! I was the winner! I loved
it—and then I found out I was the only one in my age division.
Oh well, in my heart, victory was still mine.

In Joshua chapter 6, there is victory in the story. Thick walls
had come down in the most unconventional way. The walls had
fallen flat, and the Israelites had triumphed.

Sometimes when we experience victory, we forget to give credit to the one who gave us the victory.

Very soon after this, we read of sin, which led to defeat. Joshua 7 tells us that a man named Achan stole "some of the devoted things," items that were to be set apart and dedicated to the Lord. It's telling that his sin tainted the whole nation.

Quick defeat followed the victory in Jericho. The people who had seen a win at Jericho went to fight in Ai. These were people much smaller in number. There were no thick city walls. Joshua even told the people they only needed to take about two or three thousand people, for Ai's people were few. It should have been a guaranteed victory.

SPIRITUAL HIGH

If you grew up in church, I hope you got to experience the joy of church youth camp. Or even just a weekend youth retreat. The extrovert in me lived for these. Get a whole bunch of friends together and spend the week playing silly games, eating camp food, which usually involved an excellent cereal bar, having a way too energetic camp counselor—this was my idea of heaven.

If you went to camp, you know the term "camp high." This is what happens when you have spent a week away from the world, had a great camp pastor and worship, and those youth group huddles at night where everyone bared their souls. We were filled with the Spirit, the Word, and worship. And then you had to go home.

It's unbelievable how quickly that mountaintop feeling would lead to the spiritual valley when you left the camp bubble and returned to life on Monday.

Or maybe you never went to camp or you did and had a less-than-positive experience. Think instead of a time you were at a concert or were moved by a dynamic speaker. Maybe you went on an overnight women's retreat. Stay with me. The point is that we may have times of a spiritual high that can go flat when we get back to ordinary daily life.

The Israelites had gone quickly from the heights of success to the depths of despair. What happened?

Sin happened.

Achan had taken some of the devoted things and tried to hide them. The people of Israel, affected by the sin of one, were experiencing defeat as a result of this. "And the hearts of the people melted and became as water" (Josh. 7:5).

Failure can lead us straight into the fear that we will never experience victory again. This fear can lead us to not wanting to say yes to God ever again.

What is our fear stop and faith step here?

The fear stop is not wanting to examine the hidden sins that are leading us to defeat.

The faith step: heart examination, confession, and repentance.

WHAT ARE YOU HIDING?

Rahab hid her family under the hope of the promise of the scarlet cord hanging from her window. The hope that God would follow through with His promises and save her and her household.

Achan did just the opposite. He was trying to find hope in hidden things. Shiny things. Objects hidden inside his tent because he was not supposed to have them, but he still found himself wanting them. Read Joshua 7:19–21 for the details about what he took and how he owned up.

Defeat is not always a result of sin, but it can be a highlighter to convict us of our sin.

As I write that sentence, I want to point out that there is a big difference between condemnation and conviction.

Conviction of sin points us to repentance and the forgiveness of Jesus. Condemnation points its finger and shames us. Let's remember,

> *There is therefore now no condemnation for those who are in Christ Jesus. For the law of the Spirit of life has set you free in Christ Jesus from the law of sin and death. (Rom. 8:1–2)*

If we are honest, we can try to hide things in the tents of our hearts that we think will bring hope. I can try to hide behind that hope. Reading this story, I paused to search my own heart prayerfully. What am I burying in my own heart that is not mine to keep?

Let's pause and prayerfully ask that question. Ask the Holy Spirit to answer, remembering that He does not condemn but convicts to bring victory and freedom.

God takes sin and disobedience seriously, seriously enough that He sent His Son to rescue us and take on the consequences of sin for us.

I am writing the chapters of this book out of order. I did not think I would be someone who did that, but it's just the way the process has gone for me. This is the last chapter that I am writing to finish the manuscript. I wanted to put off writing the chapter that talks about the consequences of sin. I mean, this passage in Joshua 7 can be a hard one to swallow.

Achan and his family end up being taken out and stoned by all of Israel.

This is pretty dramatic. God takes sin and disobedience seriously, seriously enough that He sent His Son to rescue us and take on the consequences of sin for us.

Instead of having to fear sin bringing the consequence of death, I can run to Jesus, who took on death for that sin.

The night before I began typing the last words on this book, I had just told my friends what a peaceful process it had been for me. How it felt like typing the words felt like an opportunity to worship.

You know how the Israelites went from victory to defeat in one chapter? From Jericho's walls miraculously falling to a tiny army bringing defeat?

I experienced that from singing the praises of writing victory with my amazing Tuesday night Bible study women (shout out to my friends who have been meeting with me on Tuesday nights for eleven years now!) to feeling paralyzed by fear the next day.

Writing a book can feel a bit like walking into a crowded room naked. (To be accurate, I have never done that!)

All I could think about was what if people don't like the book. What if I fail the fantastic publishing house that took a chance on me? What if I disappoint God? What if . . . what if . . . what if?

I was overwhelmed by lies, particularly the enemy's screaming lie that I would experience rejection, and I needed to do everything possible to protect myself from that rejection.

Like maybe take my yes off God's table.

I went to church on Sunday, and when my brother-in-law got up to preach, the title of his sermon was "Rejection." It was clear the Lord would speak right to my area of fear and defeat.

Todd said something that caused me to pause and think. "Rejection reveals our obsessions."

What was my obsession? My own name, my own reputation, my own abilities. Obsessed with being accepted and looking valuable to others. (Is now a good time to ask you for a five-star Amazon review?)

I may not have been stealing gold, silver, and beautiful cloaks and hiding them under my tent as Achan did, but I was hiding my own obsessions and pride in the tent of my heart.

If we confess our sins, he is faithful and just to forgive us our sins and to cleanse us from all unrighteousness. (1 John 1:9)

I had to have a good old prayer time of confession that morning at church. It helped to have the fantastic worship team leading in song as I prayed and confessed my pride, fears, my obsession with pleasing people over pleasing God.

Your hidden sins may be completely different than mine. Sin keeps us from following the adventure of yes that God has planned for us. It keeps us from settling in our promised land–living. It brings in defeat instead of victory.

I love this quote from my friend Wendy Blight in *I Am Loved: Walking in the Fullness of God's Love:*

> The thing about sin. It rarely travels alone. It brings with it unwelcoming traveling companions like shame and guilt. They announce their arrival something like this: There you go again. You'll never change. Why do you even try? You'll never be good enough. God will never use you.
>
> Help, hope, and healing only come when we identify the lies and expose sin's unwelcome accomplices.[10]

Let's confess our sins. To God and to each other. Walking in victory, not in defeat.

THE VALLEY OF ACHOR

When you think about a dramatic stoning, it's no wonder they called the place where they stoned Achan the valley of Achor. The

Hebrew meaning for the word Achor is trouble. The valley of trouble. That's where the enemy wants us to stay.

Stuck in the valley of trouble.

But we serve a God who wants to turn the valley of trouble into a doorway of hope.

Have you ever been stuck in a dark place? When I think about being stuck in a dark place, I remember my days leading caving trips as a summer camp counselor.

This girl who probably should not have been a lifeguard that summer for sure should not be overseeing kids in a dark cave underground. Sure, we had all the right gear. The helmets. The headlamps. The safety talk before we went in.

I hated it. I didn't mind the getting muddy part. When I say we got muddy, I mean *real* muddy. Like finding mud in your fingernails for weeks and coming-out-a-different-color-than-you-went-in-muddy.

It was very tight places in the dark that I did not enjoy. And having to try to find my way around, leading the kids through the small dark muddy tight spots.

> The same God who created light out of the darkness, in the beginning, can bring light into your darkness.

There was a part when we were supposed to instruct all the campers to turn off their headlamps. Did you know that a cave is the only place in the world that has complete natural darkness?

The kids were supposed to turn their lights off as we sat in the muddy innards of a dark cave, and I was supposed to give them a very inspirational talk about how God is light and in Him, there is no darkness at all. How we are instructed to be the light of the world, a lamp that cannot be hidden under a basket.

I believe all that and all, but I didn't want to stay in the dark long enough to take a deep dive into teaching that. You want to talk about fast-talking. As a speaker who can quickly get long-winded if I let myself, this was not a long-winded speech.

I would speak at super speed and have them turn on their lights because I did not like the darkness.

There is *nothing* like the end of the caving trip when you come toward the cave's opening. You could see the light streaming. I had to keep myself from loudly shouting glory because I was supposed to be modeling to the kids that this was a fun adventure after all.

I can still sense that relief that I would feel when I saw the cave's opening with the light streaming in.

Defeat from sin can feel like a dark place—a place where we feel stuck. The valley of Achor— valley of trouble. Here is what I love about our God as we're told in 1 John 1:5: "This is the message we have heard from him and proclaim to you, that God is light, and in him is no darkness at all."

> I don't know what areas you feel like you are experiencing defeat, but I do know this. God offers a door of hope to you today. To me today. To us tomorrow.

The same God who created light out of the darkness, in the beginning, can bring light into your darkness. We have to ask Him.

He can turn the valley of trouble into a doorway of hope.

The book of Hosea tells an incredible story that represents God's redeeming love. Hosea, a prophet of God, is instructed by God to marry a prostitute.

This was to represent the unfaithfulness of the Israelite people as God's bride. The Israelite people had been unfaithful. The Bible describes this in some pretty racy details at the beginning of Hosea 2. But then you get to verses 14 and 15. I am so excited about this I can hardly contain my fingers as they type.

> *Therefore, behold, I will allure her,*
> *and bring her into the wilderness,*
> *and speak tenderly to her.*
> *And there I will give her her vineyards*
> *and make the Valley of Achor a door of hope.*
> *And there she shall answer as in the days of her youth,*
> *as at the time when she came out of the land of Egypt.*

You should keep reading in Hosea. It's some good stuff.

I picture this verse when I think about escaping the dark cave. How it felt to see the light in the opening. A door of hope.

Friend, I don't know what areas you feel like you are experiencing defeat, but I do know this. God isn't going to stone you and leave you in the Valley of Achor.

He offers a door of hope to you today. To me today. To us tomorrow.

Hope that we can come to Him, ask forgiveness from Him, and receive the gift of redemption from Him.

Once you run into the light, you will not want to stay stuck in the dark.

Part of putting our yes on the table before God is allowing our hearts to be examined by God.

Where am I placing hope in hidden things? Where am I trying to find hope? What am I trying to hide? Let's run to His light together.

Confession. Repentance. Moving from darkness to light. Let's say yes!

MY YES PRAYER

Jesus, thank You that You are light and in You there is no darkness at all. Thank You that You can turn the valley of trouble into a doorway of hope. I want to place my yes before you.

*Lord, my yes today that I am laying on the table is allowing You to search my heart. To reveal any places of hidden sin in my heart. "**Search** me, O God, and know **my heart**! Try me and know **my thoughts**" (Ps. 139:23).*

Lord, today I confess:

Thank You that there is no condemnation in Christ Jesus. Help me to turn from the defeat of sin and walk in victory.

HEART WORK

Read Joshua 7; Psalm 139:23; Romans 8; 1 John 1:9; Hosea 2:14–15.

What is God speaking to your heart as you read?

What is one fear stop currently in your heart?

What is one faith step you will pray about taking?

Flip-Flops, Mountains, and Altars

I AM A MOUNTAIN-LOVER. I enjoy sticking my toes in the sand and spending a week at the beach, but if I had to pick a place to live, I would choose mountains any day.

There is something about the view from the top of a mountain that gets me. I will never forget the time that I climbed Mount Fuji in Japan.

I am not a detail-asking type. If you call me up for an adventure, I am generally all in, and I don't ask any questions. I also am not known as an expert in geography. So when my friends planned to climb Mount Fuji when I was spending the summer in Japan, I was ready.

It should have been my first clue that we had to start at three in the morning that this was no ordinary mountain climb. I wish I had googled things like, does the climate change as you get closer to the top? because I would have known that yes, in fact, it does and that my shorts and T-shirt without a backpack with jackets and pants in it was not a good idea.

I also should have googled appropriate footwear to climb the mountain. I will give you a pro-tip. Five-dollar flip-flops from the clearance section at Old Navy are *not* the recommended footwear.

I was determined to be victorious and make it to the top, flip-flops and all. I didn't know it would require buying a can of oxygen once I got up there. Or that I would pay the equivalent of twenty-five American dollars for a tiny bowl of rice at the top, but I wouldn't care because I was freezing and had not packed any snacks.

I would have thought there would be a beautiful view from way up on top of that mountain, but we were so high up that all we could see were the clouds.

I had hiked into the clouds. Did I mention in flip-flops? I had no idea what the adventure coming down from the clouds would be. Tiny volcanic rock makes up the terrain, and I turned it into downhill skiing—without the skis.

My legs still hurt thinking about this experience. But I did it. I climbed to the top, and I had the hiking stick where they burn a notch at every checkpoint station that you make it past. This was my remembrance of getting to the top of that mountain.

In Joshua 8, we find the Israelites on the top of a mountain. I am not sure if they were in their flip-flops or not, but here they are on Mount Ebal. Let's join them there.

They had just experienced victory after defeat. After the whole situation with Achan, God had called them back to Ai, the very place of their failure. God was reminding them He can bring victory. After the win, they came together. They may not have had a hiking stick with burned notches in it, but they did build an altar. An altar of renewal.

ALTAR OF RENEWAL

In Deuteronomy 27, Moses had already given instructions on what to do when Joshua would lead the people to Mount Ebal: Build an altar to the Lord your God, an altar of uncut stones. On the stones, write the word of the law.

This altar was different from the altar of remembrance built after crossing the Jordan River in Joshua 4. The priests picked up those stones from the Jordan to remind the people of the miraculous power of God.

This altar was an altar of renewal by reminding people of the law of God. The law of God reminded them of the person of God. He is a covenant-keeping God.

Everyone was there for the occasion. We learn that "there was not a word of all that Moses commanded that Joshua did not read" (Josh. 8:35). I love this detail that the Scripture tells us—the women and the little ones were there, as well as others who lived with the Israelites.

I love that this happened following the victory of Ai that came after the defeat of Ai. The enemy wants us to stay stuck in defeat. Fear of staying in defeat and never finding victory in our sins or circumstances will keep us stuck. We can find faith at the altar of renewal, where we remember the law of God.

> I want to say yes to God, but I am afraid of failing God.

I want to say yes to God, but I am afraid of failing God.

Here we are at that altar of renewal. Let's remind ourselves of the person of God.

You might remember way back before the exodus—at least forty years before these events at Mount Ebal—when Moses was called to place his yes on the table before God at the burning bush in Exodus 3, He asked God who he should tell the people sent him. "I AM WHO I AM" (v. 14).

God's name? I AM. The God of Abraham, the God of Isaac, the God of Jacob—this is our God.

The same God who worked in the life of Abraham, Isaac, and Jacob is the same God working His covenant-keeping promises out in our lives.

HOW ARE YOU STANDING?

We are more than halfway through the journey of this book. The journey of placing our yes to our God. How are you doing?

Maybe you feel like the Israelites did the first time they were unable to find victory over Ai's people. Your heart is melting in fear of the next steps.

Maybe you have taken some faith steps and seen some victory like the Israelites did over Ai's people in Joshua 8. Your heart is excited by what you have seen God do.

Maybe you are standing in your flip-flops on a typical Monday, wondering where God is working as you wash the dishes and do the laundry for your family yet again. Or when that project at work just grows and you're losing confidence that you'll ever complete it. Maybe it's a relationship issue that's just not improving.

It might help if you climb up that situation like it's a mountain. It will at least make you smile. Pretend I am handing you the wooden hiking stick with your victory brand burned in it.

> Learn about the names of God that represent His character. Names like Jehovah Jirah, the God who provides. El Roi, the God who sees. Jehovah Nissi, God our banner.

Wherever you find yourself, let's take a second to build an altar of renewal.

Think about the names of God that represent His character. I encourage you to study up on this. Google it, find a Bible study that teaches the names of God. Names like Jehovah Jirah, the God who provides. El Roi, the God who sees. Jehovah Nissi, God our banner.

He is God, so we do not have to be. He is God, so we *cannot* be. He is in control, and He is our victory.

The God of Abraham, Isaac, and Jacob—the Great I AM, this is our God.

RED ROVER

Do you remember the elementary school game Red Rover? It probably has been banned in elementary schools now due to insurance regulations.

I used to have a love-hate relationship with Red Rover. In this game, you have two sides. You line up shoulder to shoulder on your side and link arms. The arms swing as you yell out, "Red Rover Red Rover, send _____ right over." You call out their name, and they run and try to break through the linked arms.

I loved yet hated it when they called my name in Red Rover. There was that moment when I would try to build up the momentum to break through the other side. My non-athletic self usually couldn't get that momentum, and I ended up tangled in the swaying arms without breaking through the arms.

The end of Joshua 8 reminds me of the game of Red Rover.

One group is standing in front of Mount Gerizim, and the other group is standing in front of Mount Ebal.

One group yelling curses, the other yelling blessings.

It works. When we were in Israel, our group did just that:

half in front of each mountain, all yelling. I wanted to be the group yelling the blessings. It was crazy how the valley between caused the voices to echo, and you could hear the blessings and the curses.

Why did they do this in Joshua 8? Because they had been told to by Moses in Deuteronomy 27. They were yelling what would bring a blessing and what would bring a curse.

The blessing would come from faithfully following the Word of the Lord. From saying yes and taking the obedient faith steps that came with the yes.

Curses would come from disobeying the Word of the Lord. From getting stuck in sin and defeat and missing the Word of God.

The blessing was in hearing the Word of the Lord and following the Word of the Lord.

God is a Good Shepherd. We can trust His voice as we follow like sheep follow a Shepherd.

> *The LORD is my shepherd; I shall not want.*
> *He makes me lie down in green pastures.*
> *He leads me beside still waters.*
> *He restores my soul. (Ps. 23:1–2)*

Saying yes to follow Him leads us on a journey to our promised land.

The enemy, the thief who comes to steal, kill, and destroy, is continually trying to call us to his side of the mountain—the one that is yelling out the curses. Like Red Rover, he is trying to call us over. And once we get over on his side of the mountain, he wants us to feel stuck there. Jesus says this about him:

> *"He was a murderer from the beginning, and does not stand*
> *in the truth, because there is no truth in him. When he lies, he*

speaks out of his own character, for he is a liar and the father of lies. But because I tell the truth, you do not believe me." (John 8:44–45)

Jesus is the one calling out the blessings.

"If you abide in my word, you are truly my disciples, and you will know the truth, and the truth will set you free." (John 8:31–32)

Part of our yes to God today can be speaking the truth of God to our hearts.

Do you find the enemy speaking lies over you as you look in the mirror? As you deal with your children? As you take on that work project and then feel all the lies of inadequacies?

As you are trying to believe that God will provide for that which He has called you to while the enemy wants to tell your heart that God has forgotten you.

The enemy wants to speak curses.

Let's link arms today with one another and the truth. Shout back to the enemy the blessings—the Word of God declaring the promises and power of God.

I would love for you to write down a lie that the enemy has been speaking to your heart. Then find truth in God's Word that refutes that lie. If you would be so bold, share that with us on social media using #myyesisonthetable so we can link arms and believe the truth together.

MY YES PRAYER

Today, God, I am building an altar of renewal in my heart. I praise You that You are I AM—that the God of Abraham, Isaac, Jacob, and Joshua is my God.

Lord, I worship You from this altar of renewal. Thankful for the Word of God that changes us as the people of God.

I want to seek after Your Word of truth.

A lie that the enemy has been shouting at me is:

The truth that I am going to believe that sets me free, from Your Word is:

Thank You that You are a Good Shepherd. Your sheep know Your voice. I want to be a sheep who follows Your voice as I put my yes on the table before You.

HEART WORK

Read Joshua 8; Exodus 3; Psalm 23; John 8:31–45.

What is God speaking to your heart as you read?

What is one fear stop currently on your heart?

What faith step will you pray about taking?

Praying Big

ADELINE MAE. That is the name of the four-day-old precious baby girl that I got to hold today. She was born to my friends Casey and Barry, the friends I told you about way back in chapter 2. The ones who had experienced the heartbreaking pain of infertility and pregnancy loss. The ones I said I would hold hope for them when they couldn't.

Today I held the answered prayer to that hope. As I looked at her adorable cheeks and held her tiny fingers, I couldn't help thinking about this chapter. This chapter that is about praying big prayers, asking God to do what feels impossible.

I can find myself wanting to pray safe generic prayers instead of bold specific prayers because . . . what if God doesn't answer?

What if I'm disappointed? What if the answer is no or not yet?

These are genuine questions I wrestle with, and I imagine you do as well.

I prayed big prayers over Casey and Barry. I dreamed with them. I cried with them in the loss and heartbreak in between. I wondered when and how God would answer.

After years of these prayers, here I was holding the answer. Adeline Mae.

I share this story with a tender heart toward those of you who may be in the middle of a similar situation. Or maybe the end of your story has not turned out the same way. My heart aches for you and with you. I am praying that you sense God's presence and peace in a way that answers the prayer I am saying over you and your heart today. Prayers for comfort, a sense of God's nearness, and community to love you deep and wide.

God does not always answer our prayers in the plan, places, or ways we expect, but He always responds.

Let's pick up where we find Joshua and the people of Israel about to enter yet another battle. I wonder if the people were a bit tired of the battles as they took the land of Canaan God had promised them from the pagan peoples who populated it. I wonder if they would like to pray for victory without having to fight for victory.

I know I've been there before. I have even prayed silly prayers like *Lord, let me wake up skinny without having any evidence of the ten brownies that I couldn't resist. While we're at it, let me not have to exercise to be able to button my favorite pair of jeans.*

In Joshua 10, Adoni-zedek, the king of Jerusalem, got together a band of brothers ready to fight. (Remember that at this time, Jerusalem was not a city in the nation of Israel.) They had heard of how God was bringing victory for Israel, and they wanted to fight against that. The king of Jerusalem, the king of Hebron, the king of Jarmuth, the king of Lachish, and the king of Eglon were coming together to fight and were in it to win it.

Joshua and the "mighty men of valor" gathered for war.

> *And the* LORD *said to Joshua, "Do not fear them, for I have given them into your hands. Not a man of them shall stand before you." (Josh. 10:8)*

Some crazy things were happening in this battle. It seems like the perfect stage for a superhero movie that my nephew loves to watch. God threw down large hailstones from heaven in the middle of the battle. Talk about intense!

Joshua recognized that he needed more daylight to continue to win this battle. That's where the bold praying happens.

PRAYING OUT LOUD
IN FRONT OF A CROWD

It is a phenomenon I have seen in many Bible study groups. The ordinarily chatty group all goes mute when the Bible study leader asks who will pray aloud. No one wants to make eye contact with the leader because no one wants to be called on.

Joshua was not afraid to sign up to pray out loud in the group because he prayed a very bold, specific prayer for the battle. He didn't just pray this one silently or when it was time for prayer request say, "I have an unspoken one." He prayed in the sight of Israel.

> Joshua prayed a bold, specific prayer right there in front of everyone.

I remember those youth group days of silent requests and how it usually was a girl asking for the boy next to her to be in love with her, and she didn't want to say *that* out loud, so she said "silent" instead.

I am glad God didn't answer all of my silent youth group prayer requests. The one I would be married to right now if He answered my eighth-grade request as I wanted would mean a very different life for me now.

Joshua prayed a bold, specific prayer right there in front of everyone.

"Sun, stand still at Gibeon,
and moon, in the Valley of Aijalon." (Josh. 10:12)

I wonder what in the world was going through Joshua's heart as he prayed this prayer **out loud in front of the people.** I know what I would be thinking. I would think maybe I shouldn't have prayed quite that big of a prayer.

Perhaps I would have just said, "Lord, keep giving us strength for this battle."

Asking the sun to stand still. That is a big one.

Have you ever prayed a prayer that felt so big after you prayed it? You wondered if you should have kept that inside your heart.

I remember a time in Nepal when we were praying over a little girl we had met at the hospital. Her family brought her to us in the hospital courtyard while we were eating our lunch. She was suffering from a very high fever and uncontrollable vomiting. The doctors had said there was nothing they could do for her.

Our team gathered around this family and decided to pray. Out loud. In this courtyard, asking the God who can heal to heal. We prayed specifically and boldly for God to bring her fever down and heal whatever was causing her to be so ill.

As the prayers were coming out of my mouth, I wondered if this was too big a prayer. What if nothing happened? What if we looked like the crazy Americans who should have just gone on eating our lunch?

We prayed, and God answered. Our team watched her body immediately cool and her vomiting stop.

Right before our eyes, she became a typical two-year-old girl wanting to get out of her mother's arms and run around and play. The family was astonished, and frankly, so were we.

We ended up going to this family's home to have dinner later that week and were able to share the gospel with them. This entire Muslim family accepted Christ that night. All because of a big prayer prayed and a God who answers in big ways.

Let's go back to Joshua's big prayer. He had just asked the God of the universe to make a pause in the universe. To make the sun stand still.

And the sun stood still, and the moon stopped,
until the nation took vengeance on their enemies. (v. 13)

I love what Tony Evans says about this in his Bible commentary. "Joshua was dedicated to accomplishing the will of God—radically so. Therefore, when he boldly asked for divine drastic measures, God was willing to literally move—or in this cause pause—heaven and earth. For those who are committed to making God's agenda their own, even the wildest prayer requests just might be granted."[11]

I would rather pray big and bold and get a no than miss knowing God is answering my specific prayer in a specific way.

What is an incredibly bold and significant thing that you are afraid to pray for right now? This is a way of placing your yes on the table before God—placing your prayers before God.

WHAT DO YOU WANT ME TO DO FOR YOU?

Hundreds of years later, we find Jesus traveling through Jericho. Let's not forget Jericho's significance, where God gave a seemingly unconventional plan that caused the walls to fall.

On this day in Jericho, as Jesus was leaving, there was a great crowd. And in the middle of that crowd, sitting at the roadside, was a blind beggar named Bartimaeus. When Bartimaeus heard that the crowd was there because Jesus was there, he cried out to Jesus to have mercy on him.

Many in the crowd were telling him to be quiet. Here is where my people-pleasing would have kicked in. I would have been worried about what the people around me were thinking. I would not have wanted to be a bother. I would have liked to blend into the crowd.

Not this blind man. He wanted to see.

The more the crowd tried to quiet him, the more he cried out to Jesus.

> Fear says this is an impossible battle; don't ask for help. Faith says cry out for help to the one our help comes from. When He asks you, "What do you want Me to do for you?" what will you say?

And Jesus stopped and said, "Call him." And they called the blind man, saying to him, "Take heart. Get up; he is calling you." And throwing off his cloak, he sprang up and came to Jesus. And Jesus said to him, "What do you want me to do for you?" (Mark 10:49–51)

I have done some real soul searching reading this story. I wonder if I would be ready and willing if I were the blind man to answer Jesus. In front of all these people. To tell Him the desire of my heart. To trust Him with not only my heart but my healing.

I wonder if I would have answered generically because of fear.

Fear says this is an impossible battle; don't ask for help.

Faith says cry out for help to the One our help comes from.

And the blind man said to him, "Rabbi, let me recover my sight."

And Jesus said to him, "Go your way; your faith has made you well." And immediately he recovered his sight and followed him on the way. (vv. 51–52)

Friend, if you were on the side of the road waiting for Jesus, what would you do if He came by? Would you not want to be a bother? Would you worry about disappointment? Would you find it easier to stay in the uncomfortable than to pour out your request to Him? Imagine Jesus coming to you right now and placing His hand on your shoulder. Lift your eyes to look at Him. When He asks you, "What do you want Me to do for you?" what will you say?

THE LORD WHO FIGHTS FOR YOU

Have you ever been in a situation where you needed to defend yourself? I felt terrible for the pizza man the other day. I live in an apartment alone. (Don't worry, Mom, I'm not going to give out my apartment number here.) I will tell you that the driveway next to mine is one digit different in the address and has a tenant with the same apartment number as mine.

That tenant one driveway over likes to order midnight pizzas. The pizza delivery man has often gotten our apartments mixed up and knocked on my door with a piping hot pizza. Last week it was nearly one in the morning when I heard repeated knocking at my door that would not stop.

If I was going to go to the door at one in the morning, I needed something to defend myself. So I grabbed the only thing I could think to hold. Let's be clear, I had been asleep, so I was not thinking clearly. I grabbed my weighted blanket. After all, it weighs about fifteen pounds, and if I got enough of a twirl and whirl as I spun it around, maybe I could take out whoever was knocking on the door.

Or perhaps they would run scared when they saw my hair sticking out and my fluffy, blue-clouded robe. When I peeked through the curtains, I realized I would not need to use my ninja weighted blanket throwing skills (I mean, who thinks they can defend themselves with a blanket?), but I did need to tell the pizza man he was at the wrong house.

I really should have just taken the pizza.

Remember that Joshua prayed for the sun to stand still, and it did. The Israelites found victory. The victory was not because of them. The win was given to them. The success came because the Lord fought for them. "There has been no day like it before or since," Scripture says, "when the Lord heeded the voice of a man, for the Lord fought for Israel" (Josh. 10:14).

We have a God who fights for us. He fought the chains of death for us. Maybe you need the reminder today that God fights for you.

Like me, I imagine that you have a story where you required a defender that goes much deeper than the pizza man story. I still feel tender when I think about a time I felt desperate for the Lord to defend me.

I was active with a particular ministry, and then was asked to serve on its leadership team. I was very pleased, and was prepared to pour myself into the role.

The team met—without telling me—and the upshot was they asked me to step away from the leadership role, even before I had gotten started. No one could be specific about my apparent failings, only that I wasn't "spiritually ready" for the job. It was devastating. I spent many nights feeling like such a failure and making up all kinds of reasons why they would think I could not lead. It was a deeply painful time.

I wanted to defend myself. I wanted to fight.

The Lord did such a profound work during that season in my heart.

He kept whispering to my heart, "I will fight for you, Jenn."

I hope you are not in a situation where you need reminding of this, but if you are, may I remind you today, we have a God who fights for us.

He fought the chains of sin and death to rescue us.

The same God who fought for the people of Israel is fighting for His people today.

He is fighting for your heart.

He is fighting for your hope.

He is fighting for your healing.

He fought the grave after His death on the cross and brought victory from death to provide an invitation for you for heaven.

Joshua 10:15 ends with Joshua and all Israel returning with him to the camp at Gilgal. Do you remember Gilgal from Joshua 5? This is where the people went to heal. This is the place God showed them that He was rolling Egypt's shame and pain off of them.

Maybe you need to pause and have a Gilgal moment. Return to a place of healing. A place where God can heal and has healed. A place of victory.

Are you afraid to place your yes before God because you fear the battle that may lie ahead?

You can say yes today because you have a God who fights for you.

MY YES PRAYER

Jesus, I admit sometimes I find myself overwhelmed by the battle. The lies of the enemy can seem so much louder than the truth. Would You fight for my mind and heart with Your truth? I want to know the truth and live in the truth.

Jesus, my heart feels overwhelmed by this battle:

Would You remind my heart that You fight for me? Thank You for fighting sin and death for me. Thank You for that victory. Lord, I ask for Your strength to say yes to You no matter the battle I see before me. Help me to know how to stand still and watch YOU fight.

In Jesus' name, Amen.

HEART WORK

Read Joshua 9; Joshua 10; Mark 10:46–52; Exodus 14:13–14.

What is God speaking to your heart as you read?

What is one fear stop currently on your heart?

What faith step will you pray about taking?

10

Keep Going for the More

A FEW YEARS AGO, I PICKED UP *Anything: The Prayer That Unlocked My God and My Soul* by Jennie Allen. At that time in my life, I felt like I was living my dream. I had launched Coming Alive Ministries in 2012 and loved getting to do a mixture of counseling, speaking, and writing. If I am honest with you, I felt comfortable in my faith steps.

After all, I was living on a faith-based salary raising support (which, if you have ever experienced this, you know, saying it is comfort zone faith stretching is an understatement). I felt like having to trust God with my small bank account as a single woman was indeed faith steps enough.

When I picked up the book, I did not expect God to challenge my heart radically. To speak and ask me, *"Will you keep going for the more?"*

While reading this quote in chapter 1, my heart started down a journey I had not prepared to walk:

"I started craving . . . a reckless faith, a faith where I knew God was real because I needed him, a faith where I surrendered, obedient, a faith where I sacrificed something . . . comfort or safety or practicality . . . something."[12]

I had one of those conversations with God in prayer after reading that quote. A prayer that starts with "But God . . ."

But God, I think I have already said yes to you.

But God, I think I am already living in faith for You (after all, didn't You see my tiny bank account and big bills this month, Lord?).

But God, I am living an unconventional life for you.

Have you ever had a prayer experience like this? Reminding God of what faith steps you have already taken because that seems like surely you can stay there in those steps? In *Anything*, Jennie talks about how she and her husband prayed the surrender prayer of anything to God.

As I prayed my version of the anything prayer, I knew God was speaking to my heart. He was asking me to surrender to do anything, go anywhere, and minister to anyone at any time.

To place my yes on the table.

Again. And again. And again.

MOUNT HAZOR MIRACLE

I am terrible at geography. When I said yes to going to live in Nepal, I had no idea how to tell you where that was on the map.

It can be easy to get lost in all the cities mentioned in the Old Testament of the Bible because of that whole geography thing.

When I was visiting Israel for the first time, I will not say that Mount Hazor was at the top of my list of places that I longed to see. I am not even sure I had paid attention to Mount Hazor in the Bible before.

David Disney, the leader of our trip, knows how to plan a trip to Israel in such a way that you pack in everything. He had been to Israel many times before but had never had a chance to visit Mount Hazor, so he was thrilled to add this to our itinerary.

I tried to get excited with him, but I thought of all the more famous sites I wanted to visit. That is until we reached our destination. We walked up and looked into a vast valley as far as the eye could see. The area is untouched. There seemed to be a holy stillness in the air as our guide read to us from Joshua 11.

There is something that happens when you read a passage of Scripture standing in that place. Geography suddenly comes alive. I will never forget that after we finished reading Joshua 11, our guide was emphatically saying, "He who controlled this valley controlled the land."

The Israelite people under Joshua's leadership had already conquered southern Canaan. They had seen victory. They were walking in victory. And I imagine they might have just wanted to rest and enjoy that victory.

But there was more.

I can want to settle for one victory. To pitch a tent in that victory. I remember when I completed my first and only marathon. (I try to throw that fact out as many times and ways as I can in a conversation. For a long time, I wore the shoes I ran in with the shoe tag from the marathon because I was hoping random strangers in the grocery store would ask and I could tell them, "Why yes, this is from when I ran a marathon.")

I had not adequately trained to run a marathon. But it seemed like a great idea because it involved not only running a marathon and fulfilling a dream but doing it in the happiest place on earth, Disney World.

It was fun. Until it wasn't anymore, which happened around mile 18. Sure, we stopped to take pictures with every Disney character along the route and were running through the parks, but I was no longer having fun.

That finish line seemed so far away and like something I would never cross. The winner had probably already completed the race, taken a flight back to his home country, and had a banquet given in his honor by the time my sister and I rounded the last mile to the end.

I will never forget that moment when they called out our names over the intercom as we approached the finish line and Donald Duck placed a medal around our neck.

My legs nearly collapsed, and I could not stop crying because I had experienced victory.

I translated running and finishing that marathon to mean I never had to exercise again.

One victory meant rest for me.

That is not how it works. I could not stop exercising for the rest of my life simply because I had experienced one victory in my life.

Scripture compares our spiritual life to a race.

> *Therefore, since we are surrounded by so great a cloud of witnesses, let us also lay aside every weight, and sin which clings so closely, and let us run with endurance the race that is set before us, looking to Jesus, the founder and perfecter of our faith, who for the joy that was set before him endured the cross, despising the shame, and is seated at the right hand of the throne of God. (Heb. 12:1–2)*

It's the very beginning of the year as I type out these words—the time of year when New Year, New Me is the slogan. When everyone starts the juice cleanse, the diet plan or "what I resolve this year" posts on Instagram.

I want to run the spiritual race with victory, but I can't stop just when I think I have come to one place of victory.

BACK TO MOUNT HAZOR

Let's go back to the visit to Mount Hazor. I found a private place on the mountain, slightly away from my group, and had the most unexpected moment with the Lord.

I had tears streaming down my face as I gazed over the valley. I looked over the vast expanse of land and thought about how the Israelites could have settled for victory in southern Canaan and missed out on how God wanted to reveal Himself to them in the successes He had planned for them in northern Canaan.

Taking control of this piece of land must have looked impossible. Overwhelming. Scary. A battle plan that would surely end in defeat. In Joshua 11, the Israelites encounter an alarming enemy described as "a great horde, in number like the sand that is on the seashore" (v. 4).

> What if I am inadequate? What if I do not have what it takes? What if I do not have strength for the battle?

The Israelites had been in battle before, but this time they were facing an enemy who had better resources. Not only were they outnumbered, but they were out-resourced. Not only had several kings banded together to fight Joshua's army, but the Canaanites had chariots made with iron. This battle would have been the first time the Israelite people would encounter this.

Hundreds of years later, David would write, "Some trust in chariots and some in horses, but we trust in the name of the LORD our God" (Ps. 20:7).

When I say to a group, *I want to say yes to God, but I am afraid of* _____, one of the primary responses that keeps coming back over and over is, what if I am inadequate? What if I do not have what it takes? What if I do not have strength for the battle?

Standing on Mount Hazor, I could imagine the Israelites struggle with those same questions. Those same desires to go back and stay in the victory from before instead of seeking God for the more, the next place of obedience, the next yes steps.

Their faith steps: Go into the battle. "And the LORD said to Joshua, 'Do not be afraid of them, for tomorrow at this time I will give over all of them, slain, to Israel'" (Josh. 11:6). God even said they would burn up their chariots.

God reminded Joshua of His power. Of His promise to give them victory. I need a reminder in this moment of God's power, so I imagine you might as well.

He promises us His presence.

"And behold, I am with you always, to the end of the age."
(Matt. 28:20)

He promises power for the battle.

For the weapons of our warfare are not of the flesh but have divine power to destroy strongholds. We destroy arguments and every lofty opinion raised against the knowledge of God, and take every thought captive to obey Christ. (2 Cor. 10:4–5)

What is your Mount Hazor? Where do you sense God calling you to say yes next? Can you whisper an anything prayer to God?

ANOTHER MOUNTAIN

I will never forget the moment. It was weeks after I had prayed the anything prayer. I was staying at the house of a friend whose mom had just passed away that week.

When I woke up from my night of sleeping on the sofa, I reached over and picked up my phone.

As I lay there, I scanned Facebook, and I saw a post from a friend who lived in Nepal. She described how she had laid her body over her children's bodies and begged God not to take them as the building around her shook and crumbled.

The long-predicted big earthquake had hit this country I loved, the place I had lived for two years, and left a considerable portion of my heart with the people.

I quickly flipped on the TV news and barely found my breath as I looked at the places I had called home destroyed. In rubble.

I knew God had answered my anything prayer. I had to go. I had a degree in trauma counseling, and I speak fluent Nepalese. It was a whirlwind of activity as I quickly raised the money, bought a plane ticket, and got ready to try to offer hope beneath the rubble.

Now here I was in a village on the side of the mountain in the epicenter of where the earthquake had rattled these precious people's whole lives.

The entire village had gathered outside around the rubble because they heard someone was coming to offer them hope.

I had never seen such terror in eyes before as a large earthquake aftershock rattled the ground. They were desperately searching for something solid to hold on to. And not just physically, but emotionally as well.

I looked into their traumatized, terror-filled eyes and wondered how in the world I could offer hope here.

I looked at the wreckage and fell to my knees.

Where was God here?

While on my knees, wondering how I could offer hope to the village that day, I looked at the remains of the church that was right beside where I knelt. The people had been holding their service that day when the earthquake rattled their world. Many had not made it out of the building alive.

As I looked at the rubble, something caught my eye. There was the cross. The cross that had been on top of the church building was now among the debris. The Lord spoke to my heart at that moment. "Jenn, there is always hope beneath any rubble—it is the cross."

> Jesus carried His cross for you. He carried it so He could carry you. You are not too heavy for Him. Your fears, your hurts, your hang-ups—they are not too much for Him.

Maybe you are scared to say yes to God because of the rubble you have seen in your own life. The ground was stable, and then it wasn't. A circumstance shook you to your core, and all you can see is the ruins around it.

Where is God here?

The Lord was with the Israelite people on the side of Mount Hazor. The Lord was with me on the side of that mountain in Nepal. And the Lord is with you.

May I remind you today of another earthquake and another hillside?

So they took Jesus, and he went out, bearing his own cross, to the place called The Place of a Skull, which in Aramaic is called Golgotha. There they crucified him. (John 19:16–18)

Jesus carried His cross for us. For you. He carried it so He could carry you. You are not too heavy for Him. Your fears, your hurts, your hang-ups—they are not too much for Him.

He is our hope when the world is shaking.

He is our peace when our mind is spewing.

He is our comfort when our hearts need healing.

He is the one we can say yes to because He is the one to whom we can entrust our hearts.

GIVE ME THIS HILL COUNTRY

Joshua 13 starts with the reminder that he isn't getting younger. I am not sure that needs to be in the next greeting card happy birthday line. The Lord has another reminder for Joshua: "You are old and advanced in years, and there remains yet very much land to possess" (v. 1).

I will not go into all of the city names and places because if you are like me, you'll pretend you're listening, but you'd be thinking about a thousand different things as I recite a list.

The gist: They still had some places to conquer in the promised land. The listing of the land allotment continues in chapter 14 until we find a pause in verses 6–13. In these verses, Caleb enters the scene.

Caleb was one of the original spies sent to check out to the land during the time of Moses. In Numbers 13, we find all of the spies returning with a fear report, except for Caleb (Num. 13:30).

Reading about Caleb wants me to be a Caleb. I want to be the one who says, "Let's go!" However, there are times when I say, "I don't want to go!" When I sense God calling me into the new or the next, I can prefer to retreat into the safe and the same.

I can list all the reasons that I am not enough for this, so I cannot say yes to that. My fear stops begin to sound like this: What if my yes steps for God do not work? What if I fail? What if I am inadequate? What if I do not have the strength for this battle?

In Joshua 14, we find Caleb chatting with Joshua.

> "The Lord has kept me alive, just as he said, these forty-five years since the time that the Lord spoke this word to Moses, while Israel walked in the wilderness. And now, behold, I am this day eighty-five years old. I am still as strong today as I was in the day that Moses sent me; my strength now is as my

strength was then, for war and for going and coming. So now give me this hill country. . . . It may be that the LORD will be with me, and I shall drive [the Anakim] out just as the LORD said." (vv. 10–12)

Caleb was saying yes to God for the more. He was ready to take the hill country. He believed that the same God who gave him strength to get into the promised land was going to give him the strength to possess His portion of the nation.

Did I mention that I want to be a Caleb?

PICK UP YOUR MAT

Remember how I told you that I ran a marathon once, which made me decide that I probably never needed to exercise again?

I am serious when I tell you that I crossed that finish line and quit. I reveled in my one victory and decided I never needed to try for another. I would live in the glory of the finish line and not start walking, running, or limping toward another.

Years passed by, and I took less and less care of my body. I was living my dream, traveling around the world to speak at conferences and minister in exciting places, so there was no time to take care of my physical body.

The snack room was my favorite place at the conferences. Packed full of all the goodness you can imagine. Brownies, home-made cookies by Sister Sally, chips and pretzels—my mouth is watering even as I type.

None of these things are bad things. They are yummy, tasty, delicious things. However, the snack room became where I would run to find safety.

Maybe I had an off night speaking. I stumbled over my words. I didn't feel like I communicated the message God had for the women. I missed a whole section of my notes. They didn't laugh at the jokes. To the snack room I would run.

Maybe I had a great night speaking and saw God at work. Saw women pour to the altar and give their hearts and lives to the Lord. I wanted to celebrate that I was living this dream. To the snack room I would run.

Maybe I was slap exhausted from weeks of traveling. To the snack room I would run. Brownies and cookies with a side of chips provided the strength I wanted to experience. The more insecure I would feel, the more of my stomach I would seek to fill.

I felt stuck in a cycle of running to food, hiding behind food, and trying to get out of the endless cycle of shame and guilt that came after overstuffing myself with food. I could not imagine victory.

One day my friend Jessica invited me to take an exercise class with her. She was nervous about going and asked if I would join her there. I was terrified. I had not intentionally exercised since that marathon years before. But I reluctantly said yes.

The room temperature was . . . well, hot. I sweat even just typing those words. I couldn't figure out my right from my left. I knew none of the moves. I saw myself in the wall of mirrors, and I wanted to hide. But I wanted to learn again that I could take care of my body. So I just kept going.

> To go for the more, we have to be willing to risk.

Each time I stepped on the mat, God began to teach me, to speak to me about taking care of the physical body that He had given me. He began to teach me that I was stronger than I thought I was. That He had fearfully and wonderfully made me just as Psalm 139 tells us.

Eventually, I got this crazy sense that God was calling me to step out and take the training to become a certified teacher in that exercise method. I wanted a way to reach beyond my comfort zone and share Jesus with people who may come to an exercise class but would never step foot into a women's Christian conference. Saying this yes to God was terrifying to me.

What if I am not strong enough? What if I fail? What if I look ridiculous in that room full of mirrors?

It was a risk.

To go for the more, we have to be willing to risk.

In John's gospel, we meet a man who had been an invalid for thirty-eight years. He lay every day by the pool of Bethesda, a place where many sick and infirm would come hoping to find healing.

He was lying on his mat when Jesus came by. Jesus said to him, "Do you want to be healed?" (John 5:6).

If I were the man lying there, I would struggle between a yes and a no. What if I said yes and the healing didn't come? That could be why he told Jesus that he had no one to put him in the water and everyone else was going down before him.

But Jesus pressed past his fear. He told him.

"Get up, take up your bed, and walk." And at once the man was healed, and he took up his bed and walked. (vv. 8–9)

Saying yes to teacher training for me was a chance for me to experience healing from years of lies from the enemy.

I had a gym teacher tell me in middle school to just sit on the bleachers while the others ran because I was fat.

I had believed I would always be single because a guy wouldn't find me attractive.

I had believed that food could heal me.

Saying yes and showing up on the mat required me to lean in and listen to Jesus for His truths when the lies shouted loud.

During that first weekend of teacher training, I was terrified. I didn't want to risk. I didn't want to believe I could find healing. I was not even sure I wanted to heal.

I almost picked up my mat and went home, but not because I was walking whole. After the first intensive hours of training, our instructor told me that I was behind, and he said it in front of the others. That I was not strong enough. That I would be lucky if I ever got to teach at a community class.

I wanted to stay paralyzed on my mat that day. I wanted to go home and hide. Never come back. But God wanted me to go for the more. I silently cried, but I stayed. And I kept going back. Getting stronger. Jesus met me on that mat. Jesus poured His truth on me as I fought lies in that mirrored room. And eventually, like Caleb, I was able to say *bring on the hill country. I am strong enough.*

My hill country became teaching a community class every Saturday and Wednesday. It became showing the love of Jesus to those who showed up to class with their mats. To remind them, as Jesus showed me, "See, you are well!" (John 5:14).

Friend, where is your hill country? What is the more that God wants you to pursue?

Where have you experienced victory in the past but decided that is enough, that you do not need to walk in obedient freedom in your present? What has you feeling paralyzed, wanting to experience healing but feeling stuck on your mat?

I am praying for you as you answer those questions. I am picturing you as you wonder if you can experience more. I am asking God to reveal Himself to you just like Jesus did to the paralytic lying by the pool of Bethesda.

Look at what God says about Caleb:

But my servant Caleb, because he has a different spirit and has followed me fully, I will bring into the land into which he went, and his descendants shall possess it. (Num. 14:24)

Let's prayerfully put our names in there.

But my servant _____, because she/he has a different spirit and has followed me fully, I will bring into the land.

Go for the more.

MY YES PRAYER

Jesus, I do not want to miss the more You have for me. I acknowledge my fears. I need Your strength as I feel weak. I can see my lack of resources. I can be overwhelmed by fear. Thank You that You are my source of power.

Lord, make me like Caleb. Help me have a different spirit and follow you fully.

Lord, help me receive Your healing like the paralytic man waiting by the water. To experience You make me whole, pick up my mat, and walk into the promised land. Healed.

Show me where I need healing. Show me the more You have for me. What is my hill country?

In Jesus' name, Amen.

HEART WORK

Read Joshua 11–14; Psalm 20:7; John 5:1–17.

What is God speaking to your heart as you read?

What is one fear stop currently on your heart?

What faith step will you pray about taking?

11

Possess
the Land

I AM GOING TO START THIS CHAPTER with a true confession.
Here goes. I may or may not have smuggled a stone into the United
States when I left Israel. It has been a couple of years, so I think the
statute of limitations has expired, but just in case it has not, please
do not turn me in. I am not sure that my ministry will put up
money for bail.

I brought back this stone of remembrance because it represented
a significant moment for me. Remember how I told you that I—
who doesn't cry much—sobbed at Mount Hazor? You should have
seen me at Shiloh.

Just like Mount Hazor, Shiloh was not a city I had highlighted
in my trip brochure. I am not sure I had ever noticed that city
name in the Bible.

(I hadn't actually read the trip brochure. I am more a go-with-
the-flow, see-what-happens adventurer, and I just knew whatever
adventure it was, I was going to love it because it was the promised land).

When our bus pulled up to the parking lot, I was unprepared for what God would do in my heart there. I want to take you there as well. I will even give you a pretend stone from there.

Shiloh is a historical site in Israel that looks untouched. We reached the top of the hill, looking off over the vast valley, and our guide read:

> *Then the whole congregation of the people of Israel assembled at Shiloh and set up the tent of meeting there. The land lay subdued before them. (Josh. 18:1)*

Shiloh was the place in the promised land where they set up the tent of meeting. The tabernacle. The place where the presence of God would dwell. The people were in the promised land, and the presence of God was with them. Now what? The following sentences in Joshua 18 were what got me.

> *So Joshua said to the people of Israel, "How long will you put off going in to take possession of the land, which the LORD, the God of your fathers, has given you?" (v. 3)*

The land was ready for them. God had prepared it. He had placed them in it. He had provided it. Yet, some people were not going.

Believe. Risk. Trust.

That is what I wrote in the margin of my Bible as we stood in Shiloh.

Maybe I had said yes to God. Perhaps I had put my yes on the table before God—had taken some faith steps into the promised land. But would I stay there in what felt comfortable or keep going to possess the land?

That would require me to keep believing, keep risking, keep trusting.

To follow the same God who led me to the promised land to what He had planned for me in the promised land.

Our guide then took us to an area that could have been where the tent of meeting had been. That's where the stolen rock comes in. To explain, I have to take you to another story found at Shiloh. Before we go there, I want to ask you a question that you can tuck away in your heart.

If you were standing at your own personal Shiloh right now and the Lord asked that question of you, what would your answer be? *How long will you, _____, (go ahead and insert your name there) put off going in to take possession of the land, which the Lord, the God of your fathers, has given you?*

I believe the Holy Spirit will highlight some things in your heart. It may not be a specific place, but a plan. A person. A purpose.

It's a chance to say yes to Him again. And again. To look and see the fear stops and continue to walk in those brave faith steps.

If I asked myself this question today, my answer would be different than yesterday, but I know God is calling me to the exact three words He spoke to me at Shiloh that I wrote in the Bible margin.

Believe. Risk. Trust.

Just because you are *in* the land doesn't mean there are not more faith steps to *possess* the land.

> Just because you are *in* the land doesn't mean there are not more faith steps to *possess* the land.

One of the things that I prayed about that day at Shiloh was my calling to continue to write. I wrote that beside the words *believe, risk,* and *trust* in my Bible.

Writing was a calling I knew was part of my yes to Him, but I kept wanting to quit and give up because of rejection. I had received so many answers of no I was ready to give up, not believing

God had a yes for me. I am thrilled that God called me to keep believing His promises, keep risking and trusting because now I am writing these sentences to you.

And I cannot imagine what God is going to do through you as you say yes!

As I already shared, our guide took us to a spot that may have held the tent of meeting. That's where I stole the stone. Tiny rock. That sounds way less dramatic.

AT THE ALTAR

In 1 Samuel, we find another story at Shiloh, a story with a nice whiff of opening drama.

> *There was a certain man . . . whose name was Elkanah. . . .*
> *He had two wives. The name of the one was Hannah, and the*
> *name of the other, Peninnah. And Peninnah had children, but*
> *Hannah had no children. (1 Sam. 1:1–2)*

Any story that starts now there was a certain man with two wives has a bit of a reality TV show spin.

> *Now this man used to go up year by year from his city to wor-*
> *ship and to sacrifice to the LORD of hosts at Shiloh, where the*
> *two sons of Eli, Hophni and Phinehas, were priests of the LORD.*
> *On the day when Elkanah sacrificed, he would give portions*
> *to Peninnah his wife and to all her sons and daughters. But to*
> *Hannah he gave a double portion, because he loved her, though*
> *the LORD had closed her womb. (vv. 3–5)*

Every year they would come to Shiloh to worship God at the tent of meeting. Every year Hannah would come carrying the weight of disappointment. Of heartache. A barren womb.

In 1 Samuel chapter 1, we find her at the altar again. And she lays a hard yes on the table. A surrendered yes.

> *And she vowed a vow and said, "O LORD of hosts, if you will indeed look on the affliction of your servant and remember me and not forget your servant, but will give to your servant a son, then I will give him to the LORD all the days of his life, and no razor shall touch his head." (v. 11)*

I don't know about you, but I have had some moments at the altar myself. Lifting the depths of my heart to the one who created my heart. Wanting to open my hands in surrender but tempted to keep them closed.

Hannah had to believe, risk, and trust.

She had to believe that God was hearing her prayer.

She had to risk praying for her heart's desires in the prayers that she brought to the altar.

She had to trust God with that answer and surrender that yes back to Him, trusting His more story.

> Our fear can sometimes lead us to want to hold on to our already answered prayer. Our faith step is release and surrender, continuing to trust the one who responded to our prayer.

How can we surrender our already answered prayers? Hannah poured out her heart in belief, risked praying the desires of her heart, and trusted enough in God's answer to offer the response back to Him.

Yes, I will give my son back to you.

Our fear can sometimes lead us to want to hold on to our already answered prayer and stay where we feel comfortable. Our faith step is release and surrender, continuing to believe, risk, and trust the one who responded to our prayer.

Hannah's story of prayer and release reminds me of another son in the Bible. In Genesis 17, we find another couple desiring a son. Abraham and Sarah. God had given them a promise of a multitude of nations full of their offspring. The problem? They were in the advanced age crowd. You would find them fitting in more at a retirement center than signing up to be the room mom and the PTA president.

And actually, I would have probably laughed as Sarah did (Gen. 18:12). Laughter or not, the Promise Maker is a Promise Keeper, and we find Sarah conceiving even in her old age.

> *The LORD visited Sarah as he had said, and the LORD did to Sarah as he had promised. And Sarah conceived and bore Abraham a son in his old age at the time of which God had spoken to him. (Gen. 21:1–2)*

Isaac was the answered prayer, the fulfillment of a promise. His name meant "he laughs." Sarah was no longer laughing at the impossible but holding the one God had made possible. If I were Abraham and Sarah, I would want to hold on to him. To protect him. To keep him safe and secure. Maybe add some bubble wrap to his tent.

Have you ever experienced an answer to prayer that you want to cling tightly to instead of offering it back to the Lord in trust?

Hannah offered Samuel back to the Lord.

God asked Abraham to do the same with Isaac. To trust Him.

> *After these things God tested Abraham and said to him, "Abraham!" And he said, "Here I am." He said, "Take your son, your only son Isaac, whom you love, and go to the land of*

Moriah, and offer him there as a burnt offering on one of the mountains of which I shall tell you." (Gen. 22:1–2)

BELIEVING IN THE DARK

Have you ever had a prayer answered and had to turn that answered prayer back over to the Lord in prayer?

I remember the day like it was yesterday. I was having brunch with a mentor when I got a frantic phone call from my mom. My dad was having trouble breathing, and the ambulance was there ready to take him to the local hospital. My heart sank in my chest, and I felt anything but faith. I felt overwhelmed by fear.

The hospital happened to be only a few streets over from the café, so I beat the ambulance there. I never want to relive the moment of watching them unload my dad from the back of that ambulance and swiftly take him inside.

I felt helpless and alone. I prayed the only breath prayers I could get out.

God protect my daddy. God heal my daddy. God be with my daddy. God, I want to trust you with my daddy.

After several hours we found out my dad had two golf ball–sized blood clots that had traveled through his lungs. The doctors could not believe that he had survived. He was given a room in the ICU so he could be monitored, and we went to a waiting room. The doctor told us he would go for a simple ten-minute procedure to have a filter placed in his leg to prevent further blood clots from going to his heart.

We waited in the waiting room packed full of other families waiting.

We waited. And waited. And waited.

Maybe you are in a waiting room right now? Literally or emotionally—waiting in the dark, asking God for light.

Hannah waited every year as she prayed at the altar for a baby. Abraham and Sarah waited for their promised son. Jesus waited three days before He rose from the dead. Waiting in the dark, believing the light would come.

> Faith is believing in the darkness what God showed you in the light.

Hours went by before the doctor came into our waiting room. Time seemed to stand still, and the room began to swirl as the doctor looked at my mom and started with this.

"This was not my fault."

It's never good news when a doctor starts like this. He then began to tell us in an impersonal, clinical tone that my dad had suffered a seizure on the operating table, resulting in him having a massive stroke. If he woke up, he would be a vegetable.

I am not sure what came over me, but it was not an evangelism strategy they taught me in youth group. I do know that faith rose in me that I did not even know I had.

I looked at the surgeon and said, "I can tell you are not a praying man, but I am a praying woman, and I am going to believe God to heal my dad!"

As I said, not the most influential evangelism strategy. Regardless, faith rose in me at that moment.

Faith is believing in the darkness what God showed you in the light.

Guess what? We saw God miraculously answer that prayer. Word quickly spread to our Christian community, and before we knew it, that waiting room filled up with people praying with us, holding us, crying with us.

We worshiped. We knelt. We waited. A nurse came and told my mom that my dad was asking for her, but he didn't want her to see him until they had taken the breathing tubes out.

It was a miracle. The brain damage the doctor had predicted—gone. His need for life support—gone. He was a walking, talking miracle.

I realize healing does not always come this way. And if that has not been your story, friend, I am so sorry. I am grieving with you and for you—with the gift of hope in our Savior and His promises that are true. Immanuel, God with us, in the waiting rooms, in the healings, and when the healings do not come.

We walked into that hospital room to my Dad grinning from ear to ear and said, "If I am a vegetable, I am pretty good looking broccoli." (He was in a green hospital gown.)

He was our answered prayer.

The next day I would have to surrender that answered prayer again. And again and again and again. A different doctor walked into the room and called our family together with the news that my dad not only had a blood clot that had traveled through his lungs, but he had a rare form of leukemia that very few people survive.

The room began to spin again—the need to surrender and pray here again.

My dad faced thirty days of an inpatient hospital stay, with daily arsenic IV drips in a new chemotherapy protocol to eliminate the leukemia. Three days in, the only other man who had that treatment in this hospital passed away because the treatment was so harsh on the body. Those were long days of having to surrender our answered prayer again and again. To believe. To risk hope. To trust God to be with us and carry us. One year of daily arsenic IV drips later, and God healed my dad from leukemia.

I had to learn that once we see a prayer answered, we still have to open our hands in surrender and offer the answer back in trust of Him, no matter the outcome.

Again. And again. And again.

Let's go back to the story of Hannah. In God's timing, she conceived and bore a son. She called him Samuel, which means "heard of God." She prayed, and God heard. Hannah followed through with her part of the prayers she had prayed. She gave her son to the Lord.

> *"For this child I prayed, and the LORD has granted me my petition that I made to him. Therefore I have lent him to the LORD. As long as he lives, he is lent to the LORD."*
> *(1 Sam. 1:27–28)*

That's why I took the stone. I wanted to remember to pour out my heart in prayer to the Lord, but surrender to Him whatever answered prayers He gives.

To trust His story with my story.

So today, friend, I am passing on a stone to you. To trust His story with your story.

FROM CATFISH TO CAVIAR
AND CHEESECAKE

Erwin, Tennessee. That is where my friends told me we were going when it was time to go on vacation with them. These friends are planning types and, well, let's be honest, planning is not one of my strengths. I'd rather go with the flow and be where the party is. When they told me that we were going to Erwin on vacation, I was along for the ride.

I was slightly confused as to why they chose Erwin. When I looked up the town, I found out the only thing they are known for is a catfish restaurant. I figured I would prepare for the best all-you-can-eat catfish experience of my life.

I imagine you have said yes to a thing or two in your life when you were not sure of the details of the journey or even the destination. Saying yes does not always come with a detailed instruction guide with the next steps of the yes. (Unless it's the instructions that come with the mattress in a box that you bought on a whim from Amazon.)

There are times when we wish that our yes came with complete instructions for the next steps. There are also times when, if we knew how our yes would affect the next and the now, we might shout no!

It came time for my friends to pick me up for Erwin. Something you should know about me is this—they call me the bag lady. I find it too organized to pack in those fancy, cute, carry-on suitcases because I am more of a throw-and-go type. They have their neatly packed suitcases, and I have a variety of bags with my rolled-up clothes. They picked up the bag lady, and I noticed they seemed to be acting strange.

I started to feel a little insecure. Did I have toilet paper stuck to my shoe or something in my teeth they didn't want to tell me?

We went out to dinner, and one of my friends casually let something slip in conversation about how we would be on a plane the next day.

A plane trip was not in the plan that I knew. We were to spend the night at my friend's house and leave the next day for Erwin, which was only about a three-hour drive away. Three-hour drives do not typically require plane tickets, and I had not bought one.

My friends exchanged glances and got all giggly and had that, "should we tell her?" glance, and they burst out, "We're not going to Erwin!"

As devastated as I was not to enjoy the world's best catfish, I could not wait to see what was next.

"We are going to New York City!"

I let that sink in for a moment, and I burst into tears. I live on a tight missionary budget. I cannot afford things like a spontaneous trip to New York City.

When I said yes to the journey of being with these women, I had no idea of the actual destination. My next thought was, "The bag lady goes to New York!"

My friends had thought of this. They knew I was unprepared for the unexpected destination. They had brought actual luggage for me. They took me shopping and bought me real New York clothes versus my "barely a step up from pajamas for relaxing in Erwin" clothes. They arranged to give me what I needed for my next steps.

God had given the Israelites what they needed for their next steps in the promised land; they just needed to take the journey.

HIS MORE STORY

Let's go back to the trip with my friends. The trip where I left the catfish life for the caviar and cheesecake.

I was probably the most enthusiastic passenger on the plane that day. After all, I went from thinking I would be eating catfish in Erwin to eating caviar and fancy cheesecake New York City. Okay, so I didn't eat caviar exactly, but I ate some fantastic and fancy food.

My friends had been planning this for months.

They paid for everything.

They provided everything. We got out of the airport in New York City and hopped in a cab. I would have been quite happy to stay at Motel 6. Imagine my shock and surprise when the taxi pulled up to the Plaza! We were staying at the Plaza Hotel in New York City. *That* Plaza Hotel. The Plaza Hotel I had seen in movies.

I tried to act all cool, calm, and collected when I walked into that hotel lobby. I wanted to look like I belonged there. But wow! I could barely resist the urge to jump up and down like a toddler, enthusiastically squealing and clapping my hands.

My friends had booked us a postage stamp–sized room there, but who cares, because we were staying at the Plaza in New York! We got on the elevator, and the bellhop took us up to our room.

I was already feeling quite swanky because, well—we had a bellhop to take us to our room.

My friend who had booked the room looked confused when they took us to the floor where the beautiful suites were located: the way-too-expensive and out-of-our-price-range suites. The bellhop turned out to be a butler named Waheed. *Our* butler named Waheed.

He opened the door to our supposed-to-be-postage-stamp–sized room, which looked like a gigantic suite for movie stars. My friend said, "Waheed, I think you took us to the wrong room. This must be a mistake!" He grinned from ear to ear and said, "You guys were so nice we decided to upgrade you!"

> What if I had walked around with disappointment because this was not the destination that I had expected? However, if I am honest, I do that with the Lord and His plans for me.

We had just been given an upgrade to the penthouse suite at the Plaza. And our butler, Waheed, would be there for anything we needed all week. There were towel animals and robes, giant beds, and fresh warm cookies. Every night, Waheed brought some treats to our room.

One night, my friends told me we were going to a Broadway

play. I did not care what we saw. I mean, it was Broadway, for goodness' sake. Imagine my surprise when, after a dinner that did involve the most sinfully delicious New York cheesecake, we stopped in front of the sign for *Hamilton*. My friend sneakily asked us to pause there and take a picture. After the picture, she pulled the tickets to *Hamilton* out of her bag. The "it" Broadway show, *Hamilton*.

It was not catfish and hometown dinner theater. It was New York cheesecake and *Hamilton*.

What if I had walked around with disappointment because this was not the destination that I had expected? This was not my plan. This is not what I had prepared to happen. Are you kidding me? I would never do that.

However, if I am honest, I do that with the Lord and His plans for me.

I expect where He is taking me. I prepare what I need for that journey. I take steps to plan. Check the weather. Pack the stuff. And get ready to go where I think I am going.

How often has God had a different destination for the plan I have for that day, for that year, for my life?

I do not want this to come across the wrong way here. Unfortunately, I am not saying that your yes on the table before the Lord will lead to life always being cheesecake and caviar.

However, what I can promise is that what He is doing is more than we could ask or imagine—and often, it looks different than we imagine. Here's what Paul prayed:

> *That you, being rooted and grounded in love, may have strength to comprehend with all the saints what is the breadth and length and height and depth, and to know the love of Christ that surpasses knowledge, that you may be filled with*

all the fullness of God. Now to him who is able to do far more abundantly than all that we ask or think, according to the power at work within us. (Eph. 3:17–20)

Fear tells us that we do not have what we need when we go on this yes journey. But truth tells us God is writing this story and preparing for us what we need.

I trusted my friends to take me to Erwin. Will I trust God to take me to the next step and provide what I need in the now?

I hear Joshua's voice echoing to the people in Shiloh.

So Joshua said to the people of Israel, "How long will you put off going in to take possession of the land, which the LORD, the God of your fathers, has given you?" (Josh. 18:3)

I don't want to miss what He has given me.

MY YES PRAYER

Jesus, I do not want to miss out because I have put off my yes to You. Would you give me courage to take possession of the promises You have for me, the places You have for me to go, and the plans You have designed me for?

I do not want to miss it.

Forgive me for the ways I can settle or think my best is better than Yours.

Here are my open hands, my open heart, my surrender.

I say yes.

In Jesus' name, Amen.

HEART WORK

Read Joshua 18:1; Samuel 1; Genesis 22. (If you want to read through the whole book of Joshua on this journey, I also encourage you to read Joshua 15–17 but as a note: it's land allotment, so no judgment if you skip that part.)

What is God speaking to your heart as you read?

What is one fear stop currently on your heart?

What one faith step will you pray about taking?

12

The Promise Keeper

DO YOU EVER MAKE PROMISES to yourself or to others that you cannot seem to keep? It's currently January as I am writing these words. The classic New Year, New Me time of year. Many of us are making promises to ourselves that we end up having a hard time keeping. Or maybe that is just me.

I promise that I am going to work out every day. I promise that I will organize that bathroom cabinet that I have to shut fast to keep all the lotions I was given as a thank-you when I spoke at events from falling out all over the place.

This January, as I made my goals, I promised myself I would do better at going to bed earlier. But then it was 5:30 in the evening, and I wanted to snuggle that warm cup of rich hot coffee, so I did. And well, that shot of caffeine ended the going to bed earlier promise.

People break promises to us as well. That can turn out to be a little more painful than the promises that we break for ourselves. Maybe you have had someone promise to be there for you, and then they were not. Perhaps your heart holds the pain of broken promises from a parent, a friend, or a marriage.

I cannot imagine that you have been alive for long on this planet without experiencing a few broken promises because we are all broken people.

Sometimes I can find myself putting my experiences of broken promises with people or myself onto the character of God. If I cannot keep promises made to myself or others cannot keep promises, how can God?

That's why Joshua 21:44–45 stopped me in my tracks. I got so excited I spilled my coffee all over me. I promise you that is a typical experience for me!

> And the LORD gave them rest on every side just as he had sworn to their fathers. Not one of all their enemies had withstood them, for the LORD had given all their enemies into their hands. Not one word of all the good promises that the LORD had made to the house of Israel had failed; all came to pass.

We need to read that last part out loud with some emphasis. "Not one word of all the good promises that the LORD had made to Israel had failed; all came to pass."

The Promise Maker was the Promise Keeper.

The promises may look different for us. It may not be a specific land like it was for the Israelite people, but the Promise Maker's character is the same.

> Every good gift and every perfect gift is from above, coming down from the Father of lights, with whom there is no variation or shadow due to change. (James 1:17)

As we continue to move forward in our faith steps, we will

continue to have fear stops. There will be times when fear gets very big and our circumstances can cause us to think God is small. This is where we pause and remind ourselves together the truth that God does not change. His character is the same. His character is good. His promises are true.

One of the great promises that Jesus left? The gift of the Holy Spirit.

> *If you love me, you will keep my commandments. And I will ask the Father, and he will give you another Helper, to be with you forever, even the Spirit of truth, whom the world cannot receive, because it neither sees him nor knows him. You know him, for he dwells with you and will be in you.*
>
> *I will not leave you as orphans; I will come to you. Yet a little while and the world will see me no more, but you will see me. Because I live, you also will live. In that day you will know that I am in my Father, and you in me, and I in you. (John 14:15–20)*

Another promise: freedom from our sin and condemnation. Romans 8:1 assures us, "There is therefore now no condemnation for those who are in Christ Jesus."

In that same chapter, in verse 11, God gives us the promise that the same power that raised Jesus Christ from the dead lives in you.

The list of promises could go on and on.

Go ahead. Pick a promise from Scripture today and ask God to help you believe it even if you are afraid. I will give you space to write it here. The Promise Maker is the Promise Keeper.

ON ELEPHANTS AND THE PROMISED LAND

I am always up for an adventure. Well, unless it involves a roller coaster ride or white water rafting. Then you can count me out. When my friends from home were coming to visit the country where I was serving, we planned some adventures.

In this country, there was a real live jungle that I had not seen yet. We found out that you could take a real elephant ride in this real jungle. The travel brochure made it look so fun. Sitting in a box on the top of an elephant traversing the wild jungle seeing wildlife. I was all in.

In case you didn't realize it, elephants are very tall. We giggled (let's be honest, mostly I giggled) as we climbed the ladder to get in the box sitting on the top of the elephant's back. Each of us grabbed a corner of the box and were ready to go.

Our elephant moved very slowly. Plodding through the jungle felt fun at first. But hours in, our plodding elephant was still plodding, but we had not seen any wildlife, only other tourists on the back of elephants who had also paid to see the wildlife. Where was it all hiding?

I never thought I would say it, but I was getting bored on our elephant ride.

That is until the elephant guide below started yelling. I quickly realized that he was yelling at me.

"*Tapailai moti cha!*" You may not know what that means, but I sure did. The Nepalese translation of this is "you are very fat." He then went on to tell me that my weight was throwing off the weight of the elephant; in other words, I was throwing it off balance.

I don't know if you have ever experienced someone telling you

> I decided I may as well go for it, so I clumsily climbed onto the elephant's head.

that you are throwing off the *weight of an elephant*, but I sure have. I didn't know if I should laugh or cry, so I chose to laugh. I laughed hard—if I was going to throw off the weight of an elephant, I wanted to do it laughing.

The guide told me that I needed to climb out of my corner of the box onto the elephant's head.

I laughed some more. I am a clumsy gal. The thought of getting out of the box on a moving elephant and landing on its head without falling off seemed like quite a stretch to me.

And let's add that this was not the Dumbo ride at Disney. There were no handles, only ears that would flap up and down quite vigorously.

I decided I may as well go for it, so I clumsily climbed onto the elephant's head. In case you don't ever have the opportunity to ride on the back of an elephant's head, I will let you know that their hair is prickly, and they *stink*.

The guide gave me a small rod and told me where to poke to encourage the elephant to go in one direction. I acted like I was paying attention, but here is what you should know. If you ever give me directions, I will pretend to listen to you, but I stopped listening after the first turn.

I nodded and listened without listening. I figured this elephant was going to do what it was going to do with or without my prodding. I was still a little bit stuck on the fact that the guide had told me that I was throwing off the elephant's weight.

Things were going okay until the elephant saw its elephant girlfriend in the jungle. Listen, I don't want to get all National Geographic graphic on you here, but I will tell you this: my plodding elephant started running. And I started holding on to those floppy ears for dear life.

I was clinging on with everything I had. I was trying to remember what the guide had taught me about guiding the elephant, but it was too late. "Things" were moving too fast.

Next thing you know, our elephant's front two legs were no longer on the ground, and I was no longer on the elephant's head but had slid right back into the box.

Go ahead. You can laugh. I am laughing just thinking about this adventure all over again.

In that crazy moment, I felt like I heard the Lord speak to my heart.

"Jenn, that elephant ride seemed dull and boring when you were in the box. It's when the guide called you out of the box that you went on the ride of a lifetime. If you will get out of the box of your comfort zone and trust Me, *cling to Me*, you will go on the adventure of a lifetime."

In Joshua 23, we find Joshua old and advanced in years. He knew his time of leading the Israelite people in the promised land was drawing to an end.

I have not in any way led you to your promised land, but in the chapters of this book, I have taken a journey with you. You have placed your yes on the table, and I pray you are moving from fear stops to faith steps, one tiny brave step at a time.

> How has God fought for you? How have you seen Him rescue you?

In these last sentences in this final chapter, I want to remind you of the same things Joshua was reminding Israel's leaders. In Joshua 23:6, he says, "Therefore, be very strong to keep and to do all that is written in the Book of the Law of Moses, turning aside from it neither to the right hand nor to the left."

Joshua was reminding the people what God had done for them, how He had fought for them, how He had rescued them. Take a pause here. Maybe get out a pen and paper here. How has God fought for you? How have you seen Him rescue you?

He sent from on high, he took me;
he drew me out of many waters.
He rescued me from my strong enemy
and from those who hated me,
for they were too mighty for me.
They confronted me in the day of my calamity,
but the LORD was my support.
He brought me out into a broad place;
he rescued me, because he delighted in me.
(Ps. 18:16–19)

Then Joshua reminded the Israelites to cling to God: "you shall cling to the LORD your God just as you have done to this day" (Josh. 23:8).

I clung to the ears of the elephant that day. Holding on and praying, my grip stayed strong. It can be easy to lose our focus on what we are clinging to with our hearts and hands. That's why it's essential to go back and remember how God has been faithful in our past. It encourages us to remember to cling to Him in our present.

It can be tempting to want to cling to people or things. To cling to dreams. To cling to our to-do lists and plans. To cling to our sense of control and comfort.

O God, you are my God; earnestly I seek you;
my soul thirsts for you;
my flesh faints for you,
as in a dry and weary land where there is no water.
So I have looked upon you in the sanctuary,
beholding your power and glory.

Because your steadfast love is better than life,
*   my lips will praise you.*
So I will bless you as long as I live;
*   in your name I will lift up my hands.*

My soul will be satisfied as with fat and rich food,
*   and my mouth will praise you with joyful lips,*
when I remember you upon my bed,
*   and meditate on you in the watches of the night;*
for you have been my help,
*   and in the shadow of your wings I will sing for joy.*
My soul clings to you;
**   your right hand upholds me.**
(Ps. 63:1–8, emphasis added)

CELEBRATE

When was the last time you paused to celebrate? I am not talking about just on your birthday, but in your every day. I would have thought I was good at celebrating until I was sitting down with a dear friend and business coach, Natalie Joy, for some goal planning for my ministry.

We made all kinds of big goals and broke them down into small steps. And at the end of the steps, she would ask me, "What are you going to do to celebrate when you finish?"

I would have thought it would have been easy for me to throw out answers to that. But I realized that I could quickly pass things by and move on to the next moment. I had difficulty thinking of specific ways to celebrate because I was on to the next goal steps and ideas.

I left that business coaching time and went to my friend's lake house to spend the week writing and working on my podcast with my dear friends Melinda and Billie.

I asked them how they celebrated, and we realized we all had the same problem, that we had a hard time remembering to pause and celebrate. We worked that weekend on some celebrating ideas. Both Billie and I found out that we had book contracts at that lake house, so we celebrated with sparklers and a jump in the lake.

Melinda worked hard on her podcast (the *Even While* podcast). We celebrated with a meal and playing on the paddleboard.

We promised each other that we would celebrate making it through 2020, the year of the pandemic where our ministries had to completely pivot by planning a trip to Billie's house in Florida in January 2021 to do some more dreaming, writing, and playing. To celebrate and talk about what God had done and dream about what He was going to do.

And that is where I am writing the final words to this closing chapter. With my friends celebrating here at Billie's house. We have cried together. We have laughed together, and we have celebrated the goodness of God together.

We even celebrated by taking a writing break in the middle of the day to "take batting practice" here in the backyard. I didn't even know what that meant, but Billie's husband, Dave Jauss, has been a professional baseball coach for years. It's not every day that you get to grab a bat (I had not held one since elementary school) and try batting practice with the New York Mets' bench coach.

> Your adventure of faith is just beginning. God has so much more in store for you.

I laughed so hard as I stepped up to the "plate." As I've already told you, hand-eye coordination has never been a gift of mine.

Dave assured me that all I had to do was follow his lead, keep my eye on the ball and listen for his instructions. My stance was horrible, my hold on the bat not right, but I was having a blast. I watched as he threw, tried to listen to what he said, took a swing, and shouted when the ball hit the bat.

I did have a few good swings until I started looking at my friends who held the camera (because did professional batting practice with a professional baseball coach actually happen unless you record it on social media? Doubtful). I perhaps forgot to look at the ball, and it hit me in the face.

I lost focus and missed.

Friends, our journey together is ending, but your adventure of faith is just beginning. God has so much more in store for you. I am so excited for you not to lose focus and miss it.

The Israelites were so like us. They quickly forgot and lost focus.

In Joshua's closing speech, he reminds the people to pause. To celebrate the goodness and faithfulness of God on their journey. To remember how He took them through this journey. Joshua even had them place a large stone at Shechem so they would remember the Lord there.

I don't think they had cupcakes at this celebration and renewal of the covenant, but I am sending you a pretend cupcake here (or your treat of choice). Celebrate what you have seen God do in these twelve chapters. In your heart. In your life. In your journey of fear stops to faith steps.

After the celebration history lesson style that Joshua gives the people in Joshua 24, he gives them a command. "Now therefore fear the LORD and serve him in sincerity and in faithfulness. Put away the gods that your fathers served beyond the River and in Egypt, and serve the LORD" (v. 14).

Joshua reminds them that they have a choice. Will they serve other gods or THE God?

It reminds me of a powerful worship service at church. The

presence of God feels thick, and your ability to connect with Him and choose Him seems as easy as following the lyrics on the screen as you sing.

> *Then the people answered, "Far be it from us that we should forsake the LORD to serve other gods, for it is the LORD our God who brought us and our fathers up from the land of Egypt, out of the house of slavery, and who did those great signs in our sight and preserved us in all the way that we went, and among all the peoples through whom we passed." (Josh. 24:16–17)*

Just like the worship service excitement, they were proclaiming that they would choose the Lord.

But what about the days when the feeling of peace and joy from a time of worship no longer lingers? What about when the study is over, and you feel stuck in fear again?

Choose. This. Day.

Like Joshua, I want to leave you with this encouragement. It is a daily choice. On the days when you forget, choose again.

On the days when you see a Jordan River obstacle, ask God to help you choose again.

When you see a Jericho wall that needs to fall, ask God to help you choose again.

On the days when you need to cling to a strand of hope, ask God to help you chose again.

On the days when you need to see the impossible made possible, ask God to help you chose again.

Saying yes is a journey. It is an adventure. Let's keep on to the Promised Land.

MY YES PRAYER

Dear God, I want to choose You. Daily. Help me to set my eyes on You as I say yes to You. To follow You and not lose focus. Thank You for the journey of these past twelve chapters.

Today I place my yes on the table again.

And tomorrow—again.

Thank You that You are my hope. That I can cling to You. That I can look to You and watch You do miracles. Thank You that in You, I am free. Lord remind me as I take this adventure that You are with me. I am following You here. Help me when I am afraid. Remind me of Your faithfulness in the past as I look to see what You have for me in this present day.

My yes is on the table.

Amen.

HEART WORK

Read Joshua 19–24 (friend, you have finished the whole book of Joshua!); John 14:15–20.

What is God speaking to your heart as you read?

What is one fear stop currently on your heart?

What faith step will you pray about taking?

Acknowledgments

TO JUDY DUNAGAN, for years I prayed and dreamed for a YES from my dream publishing house and my dream acquisitions editor—that was you. I am so thankful to be mentored by you, learn how to be a spiritual warrior from you, and call you friend and editor. Thank you for putting your yes on the table.

PAM PUGH, I could not have prayed for a more fantastic editor to shape my words so beautifully. You even made me laugh out loud as I read the edits. I will forever be grateful for your gifts with the pages of this book.

TO MY PARENTS: You lived your yes on the table. You taught me about Jesus, and you showed me Jesus. I loved growing up around our dinner table.

TO MICHELLE: The best womb mate and best friend from birth ever. You never stopped believing that I would get this yes, even during years of no. You and Todd Humbert are incredible cheerleaders, and I love watching you live your yes on the table.

TO MY TUESDAY GIRLS: Catrina, Michelle, Heather, and Lindsay, the gift of your community and love kept me going all these years, and I love our Tuesday nights more than I can say. Thanks for praying and encouraging me through.

TO MY WEDNESDAY SMALL GROUP: I love our times together. Thanks for being the best community on this journey.

TO TINA: I am so glad I got the gift of friendship with you when I said yes to teacher training. Our coffees, phone calls, and classes together have been such a gift. Thanks for believing in my dream with me.

TO CAROL KENT AND THE SPEAK UP FACULTY, this would have never happened without your excellent Speak Up Conference and encouragement and mentorship. Thank you for shaping the yes of those of us called to speak and write.

TO THE CAM BOARD: Casey and Barry Lewis, Catrina and JP Pruitt, Justin and Brittany Smith, Michelle and Todd Humbert, and Houston Gibson; thank you for putting your yes on the table to being the board of directors of my crazy calling and dream. I could NOT do it without you!

TO BILLIE JAUSS AND MELINDA PATRICK, this book would not have happened without you guys. Dreaming with you and walking out our goals together has been such a gift. I am so grateful for our times at the townhouse, the Red House, the Jauss House, and the Lakehouse.

TO CASEY, BETH, AND JANE: Thank you for Segway tours and Erwin, New York, and the memories in between.

TO DEB BROWN for being my God-sized dream sister and teaching me to be brave.

TO JESUS: You are my best yes!

Notes

1. Cambridge Dictionary, s.v. "lay your cards on the table," https://dictionary.cambridge.org/us/dictionary/english/lay-your-cards-on-the-table.

2. James Strong, *A Concise Dictionary of the Words in the Greek Testament and The Hebrew Bible* (Bellingham, WA: Logos Bible Software, 2009), 15.

3. Lara Casey, *Powersheets Make It Happen: The Intentional Goal Planner* (Lara Casey Media, 2017), 15. Also see https://laracasey.com.

4. Heather Holleman, *Chosen for Christ: Stepping into the Life You've Been Missing* (Chicago: Moody, 2018), 20.

5. Terrica Joy Smith, "Made for This: An Interview with Terrica Joy Smith," interview by Jennifer Hand, *Coming Alive Conversations*, Season 4, Episode 12, March 22, 2021, https://www.comingalive ministries.com/2021/03/made-for-this-an-interview-with-terrica-joy-smith/.

6. Joanna Ivey and Hailey Johnston, "God Works in Our Yes with Project Free2Fly," interview by Jennifer Hand, *Coming Alive Conversations*, May 13, 2019, https://comingaliveministries.libsyn.com/god-works-in-our-yeses-with-project-free2fly/.

7. Strong, 44.

8. Cindy Bultema, "Following God and Living Full/Walking Free: An Interview with Cindy Bultema," interview by Jennifer Hand, *Coming Alive Conversations*, Season 2, Episode 12, June 18, 2019, https://www.comingaliveministries.com/2019/06/following-god-and-living-fullwalking-free-an-interview-with-cindy-bultema/.

9. *Merriam-Webster*, s.v. "victory," last updated November 29, 2021, https://www.merriam-webster.com/dictionary/victory.

10. Wendy Blight, *I Am Loved: Walking in the Fullness of God's Love* (Nashville: Thomas Nelson, 2017), 49.

11. Tony Evans, *The Tony Evans Bible Commentary* (Nashville: Holman Reference, 2019), 253.

12. Jennie Allen, *Anything: The Prayer That Unlocked My God and My Soul* (Nashville: W Publishing, 2011), 9–10.

COMING ALIVE MINISTRIES

Coming Alive Ministries was officially founded in May of 2012 as a 501(c)3 with a dream and a calling to provide an invitation to Come Alive in Christ. Jenn Hand, Executive Director and founder of Coming Alive Ministries, returned home after living overseas for two years as a missionary in a country where people worshiped idols and statues all around her.

As Jenn returned home, she found herself traveling and speaking to churches about her experiences serving overseas. She began to notice church pews packed with people who said they knew the living God, but were living dead inside.

In addition to conferences, retreats and written resources, Coming Alive Ministries provides missionary care and counseling and trauma debriefing around the world after natural disasters.

Find out more at **www.comingaliveministries.com**